Re-Appraisals:

Some commonsense readings in American literature

by the same Author

A Mirror for Anglo-Saxons
Science and the Shabby Curate of Poetry
The Problem of Boston

This is the first volume in a series of essays on American studies which is
under the general editorship of S.Gorley Putt

Re-Appraisals:

Some commonsense readings in American literature

by Martin Green

W · W · Norton & Company · Inc · New York

Acknowledgements

The author feels very grateful to the staff of
the Shrewsbury branch of the Shropshire
County Library, who went out of their way,
often, to help him get the information and
the books he needed while he was writing
these essays. A version of the chapter on
Hawthorne appeared in *Essays and Studies*
(English Association, 1963); and that on
James in *The London Magazine*, January
1963

for Elsa Greene

Contents

Foreword

My sub-title will not, I hope, be taken only in its more
boastful sense; it is intended also to admit a simplicity
that may appear in these essays when they are compared
with several recent books on American literature; books
I must spend most of my time criticising, but to which
it will be a severe test to be compared. Few of my
readings are new; most of them are returns from more
exciting speculation to what I think most people –
including those who dislike them – will agree are the
obvious and 'commonsense' interpretations of the texts.

Preface to the American Edition

As it is now three years since I wrote these essays, there are of course things in them I would now not say, or say differently. The only case in which there has been any change in the substance of my opinion is the Whitman essay. I would now want to call Whitman not an important poet, but a great one — in an odd way, and not in all places, sometimes in the middle of being a bad poet. He is great sometimes when there is real confession in the poem, and sometimes when there is real dialogue between major voices, notably between the love of life and the love of death. This does not alter the substance of my argument in the essay, but it would alter, if I were now writing that argument, the accidents of tone and treatment, allusion, comparison, commentary, quite importantly; and I take it that all those are included in opinion. A great writer must be treated differently from even an important one; this is not a matter of personal politeness, or social decorum, but of the literary act itself, the essential relationship between reader and writer. I believe — it is obvious — in the dignity of the reader, his right to demand evidence for the writer's claim to occupy his mind and direct his imagination. But when that proof comes, insofar as it comes, the relationship changes. The reader is now primarily learning, dependent, a client, however much of what is done to him remains dismaying, and his response to it is importantly different. Of course he must remain critical, just as of course he should have been sympathetic before, but a big change takes place. One of those changes has taken place in my opinion of Whitman.

In the Emerson essay also I would change things, but because of its strategy, not its inspiration. I have lost faith in that way of arguing the case. I think — I hope — that if somebody else had written that essay, and I read it, I would be convinced; but I don't think anyone else would; because I associate Emerson with things and people I am strongly for or against, without being able to justify (there) either my strength of feeling about those things or my association of Emerson with them. Its method is too speculative and far-ranging; a quieter, less declarative, less enthusiastic essay, merely rehearsing some of the best things in the Journals, would have served my purpose better, perhaps. Though I am not sure; I think those who have read my other books could see the background against which Emerson takes on the significance I there assign him. But it is no doubt impudent to suggest that people should read something else in order to understand this; especially if they are already irritated by what they have understood.

Then, in the essay on Salinger and Nabokov, I would now want to guard against seeming to be simply in praise of cleverness. Clever remains an important characterizing word for these writers' methods, but it would perhaps be wise to insist more that those methods, that cleverness, derives its best interest from its relation to their seriousness — their delicacy of feeling, their range of understanding, their power of compassion. The "smartness" in each of them, which so offends our sense of the serious, is ingeniously harnessed to their seriousness, and in this they are different from most of our other clever writers. For what I call there "rococo realism" has since shown itself to be a characteristic modern resource for other writers — Saul Bellow, in *Herzog,* is a good example — and non-writers. Among film-makers, for instance, Fellini has most notably followed a mode strikingly similar to that of *Lolita* and *Introducing Seymour*. *8½* answers to the definitions of that essay very strikingly; the recording of contemporary details, the use of personal fantasy, the broken narrative method, the showy technical brilliance, the incompleteness of form, the slyly frank autobiographicalness, the inner painfulness. Many other writers have been attracted to the same mode in the last decade, sometimes against or athwart their more native beliefs or talents. Kingsley Amis, despite his preference for brass-tacks bluntness and plain-speaking, writes novels that make aesthetic sense only from a similarly special and indeed fancy point of view. Those rapid alternations of realism and day-dream fantasy, those jazzy plots and cartoon characters, are held together and made interesting only by being all parts of a tricky self-interrogation and self-punishment, carried out in full view of the reader and yet in full entertainer-anonymity; a seven-veils dance, by a man, in Trafalgar Square. Doris Lessing, surely England's other really interesting novelist, is as far as possible in temperament from Nabokov. She tries to tell the truth, simply. And yet in *The Golden Notebook* she too sets up an elaborate framework of illusion, and embarks on the trickiest kind of autobiographical strip-tease. Her real virtues do not derive at all from "rococo realism"; many characteristic vices of modern writing *do;* so if I were writing that essay now I should insist more on the other qualities in Nabokov and Salinger which make those methods fruitful for them.

But most of what I want to say in explanation of this book, or possibly in justification — certainly not in apology — is more general. Within the category essay, these chapters mark themselves off from other people's, especially essays by scholars in the humanities, by their approximation to the character of pamphlets. That is, they are arguments addressed to a kind of general reader and intended to change that reader's whole mind by giving each subject its aspect of public and urgent importance. They are not, then, intended primarily to communicate profound knowledge of that subject, or to manifest the most mature judgment of it — though of course ignorance and immaturity are faults in such work. The essays here on Emerson and Salinger intend to claim more serious attention for them, and fully to enforce that claim, but only to indicate, to illustrate, the kind of importance pure literary criticism might, after such attending, assign them. Even more decidedly, pamphlets are not intended to feed the scholar's lamp with new and perfumed oils, to further enrich the rich peace of the cloister. They are nearer to intending to destroy that peace. Partly in order to let fresh air into the cloister, but even more to douse the poisonous fumes that are emanating therefrom today and spoiling the general atmosphere. I mean the ideas about literature, about the imagination as a whole, which scholarly studies now promote.

We live in an age of alienation. Creative artists and social scientists tell us, not unanimously but in impressive numbers, that the awakened man today typically feels alienated from his society, and the unawakened man is typically alienated from himself. There is a really powerful despair somewhere in most people's imaginations; a confident and communal distrust of every expansive movement of the mind, of everything undisillusioned; a prejudice in favor of the tragic, the agonized, the seared, in every account or image of human experience that claims to be serious. Probably alienation is less new, as a phenomenon, than is suggested, but probably also it is more true of our own day than of most past ages. From the point of view of the imagination, taking that in its largest sense, it seems to me the most important fact about our cultural situation.

Looking back on what I have written, I now think it is all in one way or another a response to that challenge. It is all an attempt to argue against, and demonstrate against, that alienation and despair insofar as they disease — melodramatize, sentimentalize, hydrocephalize

— our collective brain. This seems to me true even of *Mirror for Anglo-Saxons*, where America was contrasted favorably with England precisely because it afforded the individual more grounds for faith and for hope, more encouragement to participate in general enterprises. (That America, in other aspects of her life, afforded more grounds than England for alienation and despair, was not to the point; the foreigner can pick and choose what he will see, or fully feel.) *Re-appraisals* is a protest against a literary taste and method which seems to me to sacrifice even logic and common sense in its search for early patrons of the alienated mind. *Science and the Shabby Curate of Poetry* is an attempt to identify, analyze, understand, some of the controllable sources of that despair among literary men. And *The Problem of Boston* investigates an unalienated society; one which signally failed to produce the great literature it aimed at, but one whose failure in that as much as its success interests us just because of its differentness from our own condition.

That is the public and topical urgency in the name of which my books seek to change the reader's mind — that is, his character of thought about such matters. And the form of the books as much as their content is determined by this purpose. Pamphlet-essays are not merely the quickest and easiest things to write about such a thesis; they are themselves an enactment of it, a protest, demonstration, appeal, against alienation.

Let me return to *Re-appraisals,* and the area of literary criticism, where it is simplest to point out the poisonous fumes with which scholarship spoils the atmosphere — compounds the problems of alienation, that is. If the literature of our day expresses, in significant degree, a profound resentment against the society it belongs to, a decisive disengagement from it, what response can the critics and scholars of that literature make? They are obliged to participate in that society's institutional and cooperative life — to examine, to evaluate, (literature, but also books about literature, and also students of literature) to educate, to award degrees — and ultimately to make some kind of social sense out of the poems and novels. With a literature like the modern, they face a double danger; that they will either reject the writers and lose sympathy with their work, or join the writers and lose all sense of other values. There are of course several ways of avoiding both dangers, and several ways of falling into both. The typical modern choice, massive scholarly works about shrilly rebellious writers, seems to me to do the latter. When this involves, as it has in American literary studies, reinterpreting and misinterpreting the writers of the past to make them fit the theories of alienation — the power of blackness in the American imagination — then this intellectual vice is seen at its most lurid.

Massive scholarly works can of course have intellectual vitality and cultural relevance. We need only mention Marx, Freud, Weber, to demonstrate that — and perhaps to suggest the inappropriateness of that kind of model for other enterprises. In literature one can think of Auerbach's *Mimesis* as an example of the same style triumphing. But in literature (and it is surely not alone in this) the triumphs of vitality and relevance have been quite as much the achievement of the pamphlet-essay. That, after all, is what one must call much of the work of Matthew Arnold, T. S. Eliot, Yvor Winters, F. R. Leavis. Some of their essays are purely appreciative and aesthetic, but in more there are some of the characteristic features of the pamphlet. The changing of the reader's whole mind, whole taste, the appeal away from literature itself, the invocation of large cultural causes, the use of writers and even passages of writing for the critic's own purposes — these are elements in a very noble tradition of discussing literature. Whether or not this is 'better than' the strictly scholarly way, or the purely appreciative, is not a question. It is good and necessary, and must not be allowed to seem inferior, or merely amateurish.

Today, moreover, in the situation I have described,

this tradition has special advantages over its rivals. The broadly appreciative essay, its responses free of all constraining ulterior motives, can take us deeper into the particular work of art, and the general aesthetic experience, than anything else; and we need that today as much as the pamphlet. But it cannot serve so well the purpose of protesting a whole system of taste, a whole disposition of mind. A scholarly work like Auerbach's perhaps can; it can, that is, just by its more than literary scope, have a cultural effect; but it can rarely keep its cultural motive pure and passionate, subjugated as it is to so much fact. To produce a comprehensive scholarly treatment of a major theme means resigning oneself to ten or twelve years of patient, if not brutal, labor. Your life's work can therefore be only three or four books. There is nothing to regret in this; but there is much to regret in the corollary that only on those three or four subjects can the writer speak with conviction — and that on those subjects only he can — that what is not scholarly is journalistic, what is not a ten-year volume is a book-review. Moreover, the process by which such books are produced, the vast convict workshop of scholarship, is such a dreary sight, once one turns one's eyes away from the best two per cent of those involved, that one must protest against it in some way; the sadomasochistic strain in the respect evoked by these matchbox Vaticans makes it a kind of duty *not* to take the charitable view of them, and even more not to participate in their production. Of course, that best two per cent produce some very valuable books. But, unlike the appreciative essay, the scholarly volume cannot be judged by its best representatives. "Scholarship" is a cultural fact today, an institution, a force, and has to be judged by those grosser features it fathers, those worse influences it propagates.

The scholarly volume (and this applies to esoteric myth-interpretations as well as to historical-factual studies) is surely the equivalent in literature of those huge impersonal institutions in social life, and those masses of data in the world of knowledge which are often blamed for other varieties of alienation. They make people feel that nowadays it is impossible for any one person to know or discuss more than a tiny fraction of one subject — that is, that large views can only be amateur. But if the essay is a valid way of expressing serious thought about literature — as of course it is — then the individual *can* participate in the imaginative and intellectual life of his society. He can act, in and on the situation. He can say something worthwhile without knowing everything about the subject. (By worthwhile I mean of course something more independent of the current modes than is possible in a weekly magazine.) And the pamphlet-essay is the way in which we can act on the sensitive *core* of the situation. We can take part in the typical processes of the modern mind, and yet serve the forces of life.

Alienated in some sense we certainly are. But, as so often, to assert that conclusively is to complicate and hypertrophy the problems the word set out to describe. In another sense, after all, we are not alienated. If there is a fount of despair in most people's imaginations, there are founts of vitality, too. Nor can we call all of them just survivals of earlier, healthier cultural life, or purely private achievements in personal relations. The imaginative and intellectual life of our times, the whole of the world, mediated to us through *our* imagination and *our* mind, has great richness and many harmonies. If the explicit refrain of that music, by the imaginative writers, is alienation, surely it behooves the more reflective writers to point out the participation, the vitality, the health, *im*plicit in that refrain. And it surely behooves them also to strike down the hands that come at us with chloroform pads, scholarly theories of the Decay of Mind in America, or the Death of Tragedy, insisting that only the smell of death is beautiful to a mature sensibility. These are generalities, of course. The specificities are in the essays.

American literature as a subject

Students of literature are always ready to think that their subject is in a dangerous state; that the wrong books are being read, that no one is saying the important things, that contemporary taste is seriously corrupted, that literary criticism is ceasing to be an intellectual discipline. Those who make such complaints usually need to read some music criticism, or even more some art criticism, in order to discover how healthy their own subject is. Nevertheless, it is just such a complaint this book makes; not about literature in English as a whole; but American literature, the subject, does seem to me, after I have invoked every sense of proportion and realism, in a dangerous condition. It is becoming a Tom Tiddler's ground for seekers after buried meanings, an intellectual picnic site where everyone is wearing the Emperor's New Clothes, a great bustling bazaar of symbols and theories and readings and discussions which have lost their relation to the books they allegedly discuss.

This is not to deny – quite the contrary – that a great deal of real intelligence and hard work goes into the discussion of American literature today. This is no interregnum; it is quite opposite in character to the period from, say, 1880 to 1917. Today, critical style and method in this subject have a wealth of life, a full rounded glamour of intellectual self-confidence, energy, and enthusiasm. You can tell that these writers believe in what they are doing, both as a mode of precise knowledge and as a means of grappling with ultimate problems. In a sense, this wealth, this glamour, is a symptom of what is wrong; because it derives from an interpenetration of different intellectual modes – an interconnexion established between different kinds of truth – literary, ethical, political, sociological – and this in its turn derives from an excited exaggeration of the critical function. Men of literary sensibility today feel they can recognise, and interpret, and evaluate, the total moral life of a nation, on the evidence of their reading. In another sense, however, this wealth of life is genuine health. Criticism at its best *is* exciting and excited in just this way; at its very best it involves other intellectual modes in this way, too; and the pride which puts the sheen on these writers' styles derives from a genuine exercise of intelligence. But it is an exercise that has slipped the controls of cautious relevance and the all-originating text. What is wrong with the criticism of American literature today is that the critics get to the exciting part too fast. They are too ready to interpret literary detail in terms of, not the book in which it occurs, but a general theory of American literature, or of the American psyche. This occurs overtly in books like Leslie Fiedler's *Love and Death in the American Novel*; but covertly it is there in Alfred Kazin's work, Marius Bewley's, Richard Chase's, even F. R. Leavis's. Literary criticism generally, but especially in this one section, is becoming an exaggerated discipline, reaching out into political, economic, historical areas where it has no authority; and also, by that same exaggeration, losing its grip on the actual texts.

Surely there is no other area of study in which the

theorising so overrides the data. The major texts of American literature are nowadays not so much over-interpreted as re-invented. One cannot find the books the critics talk about under the titles of *The Scarlet Letter* or *Huckleberry Finn* or *Pudd'nhead Wilson*; the criticisms of American life they attach to particular episodes and characters are often entirely their own invention; the total meanings they ascribe to the books are works of fiction in their own right. In the discussion of authors like Faulkner and Melville, not only the general tone but specific references genuinely baffle; Ishmael is a typical representative of the urban proletariat; Joe Christmas is 'Man' trying to discover the particular kind of man he is; Sophia Hawthorne's (gossipy) letter about Melville makes her an important Melville critic. In what other area of study could one find such solemn and elaborate treatments of definitively minor books – comparing, analysing, appreciating them, entering minor caveats, returning to the staple enthusiasm. Take this passage from a long discussion of *The Sound and the Fury*: 'Melville's *Pierre* suffers by comparison with Faulkner's book by the diffusion of its effect.' Surely Melville's *Pierre* suffers by comparison in this particular with almost any book ever published – though we are often now called on to shake bewildered heads over its unfavorable reception: but my point is that the judicious tone here is wildly, insanely, at odds with the judgements made. The passage continues: 'Even *The House of the Seven Gables*, a more distinguished and authentically historical chronicle of a family curse, lacks the sturdy consistency of *The Sound and the Fury*.' Again, how many novels are there which are not stronger in 'sturdy consistency' than *The House of the Seven Gables*? None of these comparisons makes critical sense; to find them all together, offered in this weighty manner, by a distinguished critic (Richard Chase), with a dozen learned references, makes the reader literally blink and recoil. There is a kind of insanity in it. Especially the beginning student may turn back to the book he has just laid down, quite seriously alarmed, sometimes, to have so totally missed what was there. If he is to stay in the study of literature, he will have to learn to find those meanings, recognise those parallels, suggest similar ones himself, and stifle, even to himself, any unworthy doubts. Then, after a few years of this, he will have students of his own. This is the picture of a subject in a dangerous state.

In this first essay my thesis will be not *that* it is so, but how and why; *why* this subject should be so dominated by excited theorising; *how* passionately committed readers have come to have such a cavalier way with the text.

I am going to offer a historical account of modern methods of studying American literature. Obviously so brief an account must be a very simplified sketch. Moreover, if it is to be an explanatory account, it must select and omit even more radically. I am going totally to ignore, among others, both Parrington and Matthiessen; and I shall have very little to say about any 'history of ideas' approach to literature, or any of the political approaches of the 'thirties. The only defence for this must be the claim that these approaches are less important in the absolute scale than those I shall mention, and that in relation to what I am trying to explain they are *much* less important. But there is no claim that they are *un*important, or that this account takes care of the subject.

It is commonly agreed that the modern period in American literature, both critical and creative, began about the time of the First World War. To a considerable degree, it was the actual experience of going to the war, the shock of seeing modern nations in battle, which destroyed once for all some deep American myths about social life and human behaviour, which demanded a fresh start in men's approach to experience. You see this directly in Hemingway's work, and the more indirect result in Fitzgerald's. Co-operative with this was the experience of living in Europe – seen now as the home of both older traditions and newer experiments in living. You see how this co-operated with the experience of war in novels like Dos Passos's *Three Soldiers*; Europe offered itself as the place where the new approaches to life could be tried out.

But in a sense these experiences only confirmed what was already known, only made practically available what was already theoretically sanctioned. The old American myth, composed equally of individualistic capitalism and idealistic culture, had long ceased to convince. In 1915 Van Wyck Brooks had pointed out not so much the ugliness of the one and the flabbiness of the other as their out-datedness; America's apparent inability to *replace* them. And he treated the idea of Europe's being culturally superior – not for containing works of art, but for containing conditions of life for free spirits – as equally well-established. The old myth, emblemised for Brooks by Bryant, Whittier, Longfellow, Lowell, above all Emerson, had in its day explained America to Americans most nobly, as the country of the future, the symbol of progress, the inheritor of an ageing Europe; but even before the war that picture of the country had ceased to seem true to the young and critical. They thought more of what had gone wrong in America, of how culture had decayed there; though they had not yet any myth of their own with which to replace the old one.

What the war years brought, then, was a fundamental insecurity, a sense of, not the inadequacy of the
American myth, but the instability of *any* social myth;
the need to use power and discipline and severity too;
the frailty, indeed the dangerousness, of bright ideas
and warm feelings by themselves. And of all such ideas,
perhaps the frailest and most dangerous was that of
progress. The future, it now appeared, would not necessarily be better than the past. There were signs that it
might be worse, especially for free spirits. The dream
of a Brave New World became a nightmare. This disillusionment profited by the contact with Europe to
learn from the right-wing reaction there; ideas like
T. S. Eliot's 'classicism, royalism, catholicism' gained
intellectual vogue, and the enthusiasm for Russian
communism was not as different in intellectual character as it was in political programme. The feeling that
more intellectual people were thinking along such lines
gave a taint of irresponsibility to the experiments of the
more naïve artists of the 'twenties; you see this in Hart
Crane's relations with his mentors and in Fitzgerald's
whole career. But this disillusionment with idealism
and experiment did not lead to any imaginative en-
dorsement of the *status quo* in America, even to the
degree it did in England and France. America was still
'the country of the future'; it was irremediably identified with progress and democracy in the most dangerous
senses; it had nowhere, unless in the Deep South, a
status quo to be reactionary about, in however sophisticated a way. Americanism in every ordinary sense was
the natural enemy of the modern literary movement, in
all its serious manifestations.

American literature as a subject, meanwhile, seems to
have begun its modern career with the publication of
three books; Van Wyck Brooks's *America's Coming-of-
Age* (1915), D. H. Lawrence's *Studies in Classic American*

Literature (1925), and Constance Rourke's *American Humor* (1931). All three are quite brilliant books, and each is quite different from the others, so one feels an injustice in any generalisation applied to them all. But from our present point of view it is striking how much they are all *not* works of literary criticism. They are books about American society, American psychology, American morality, American spirituality; taking their evidence of all this from the literature. This is so striking partly because all these writers have a profoundly and even primarily literary sensibility. They are not historians or psychologists or moralists, approaching literature through another interest. You see this not only in their very acute remarks about particular writers and books, but in their approach to non-literary phenomena. They are literary people handling their history, psychology, etc., through literature; and ultimately it is to books again that their insights can be applied with most assurance and most profit. We may say that theirs is a genuinely literary but not a critical way of treating literature.

Another striking likeness between them is their radical and prophetic treatment of the literature they discuss, inverting established reputations, revealing new and frightening forces at work beneath its bland surfaces. The America they reveal to us is a place of enormous stresses and terrible strains, moral, emotional, and social; as compared with Europe, it is not, as the conventional pictures of the country insist, more innocent, more hopeful, more happy, more relaxed, but quite the contrary; it is the home of black and terrible forces. And the books to which they directed our attention were naturally those in which these truths become evident, in however indirect a way.

In D. H. Lawrence's book we have also an example of the part the European mind has played in the establishment of this subject. Lawrence used the books he discussed, and America as a whole, as ideas, as pure embodiments of psychic forces; with less attention to their *other* meanings, less concern for their complex factuality, than he gave to, say, either England or Italy as a country. This has continued to be true of European commentators on America; they have permitted themselves a freedom of interpretation which, if applied to any other subject, would have seemed a sign of popularisation. The curious thing is that though this has naturally been resented, it has not been effectually corrected by Americans themselves. Those whose minds move on a comparable level of intensity and insight have used a similar freedom themselves. Partly because of the intellectuals' anti-Americanism, and partly because of the theoretical cast of their patriotism, America remains an idea to them, too. It is difficult, for instance, to parallel Van Wyck Brooks's tone about America in an English book about England. Thus the subject of American literature was inaugurated in the modern period under the auspices of a highly literary, but not literary-critical, method of discourse; and of a highly radical and prophetic attitude to America.

But not until much later, not until quite recently, did those auspices seem to have been effective. The three interpretative books were to the academic consciousness curiosities; to the general intellectual consciousness, they belonged to the undisciplined effervescence of the 'twenties. There were developments in the subject that paralleled their way of treating it; a discovery of Melville and Emily Dickinson, a re-interpretation of Hawthorne, an attack on Emerson; the emphasis was being put on the 'blacker' forces in the American psyche, but in a different manner and with a different effect. During the 'twenties, 'thirties, and 'forties, American literature remained a quiet branch of study, less ambitious, not more, than other branches. Critics like Perry Miller and Newton Arvin were exceptions; but they do not disprove the rule. The work done was often surveys and catalogues of unexciting books, appreciated in a quite humble and parochial spirit; and under the general heading of 'American Studies', or 'American Civilisation', literature was studied in the spirit of history or sociology more often than the other way round.

The most exciting work in literary studies during those years was that of the New Critics. This group can of course be defined in such different ways as to include quite different people; but from our present point of view, Kenneth Burke, R. P. Blackmur, William Empson and I. A. Richards were all on the fringe, and the core of the group was John Crowe Ransom, Allen Tate, Cleanth Brooks and Robert Penn Warren. Their work was quite opposite in character to that of the three interpretative books. The New Critics were purely and professionally literary critics; they were interested in poetry more than in fiction, or prose at all; they were interested in formal qualities, not psychological or sociological content; they were comparatively uninterested in American literature, and in the centuries represented there. Nevertheless, they have profoundly influenced the shape that study has now taken; because they formed the literary mind in America.

They were the most distinguished inheritors of the disillusionment. The Southern Agrarian manifesto *I'll Take My Stand* was a protest against industrialism, scientism, liberalism, protestantism, progress – 'everything abstract and abstracting'. Its authors wanted a 'stable, religious, agrarian' society; a way of life with dignity, courtesy, leisure, that grew unbrokenly out of the past. The word 'tradition' sums up nearly all of it; the interpenetration of particular economic, aesthetic, social habits; which implies also the interpenetration of particular families and farms, names and places. Industrialism was decomposing tradition, separating off the different areas of our experience, making the arts impossible; our culture was being atomised. And, part cause, part consequence, the scientific mode of knowledge dominated our consciousness, the aesthetic was neglected. Contemporary America, therefore, the immediately present, was the apotheosis of everything to be resisted.

And in the way all this was written, the elegant allusiveness, the irony, the mock-biographies, the personifications, the dialogues, the combinations of the precious tone with the assured seriousness, one finds the tactics of resistance. One finds the literary future. The mind we know so well, that mind whose thoughts for so long answered all our efforts at reflection, is there. Elegant, erudite, indirect, severe, insisting on decorum, meeting the world with 'strategies', dealing with experience always draped in some stage-property, from some historical pageant; never simply, nakedly passionate, never personal, never 'romantic', or 'enthusiastic'. It is a mind quite fundamentally opposed to most things that have happened in America since the Civil War, and to most personal qualities by which the outside world, at its friendliest, identifies the American. The alienation of the literary mind from its social environment is no doubt too general to characterise one particular mode, but this was programmatic and almost dispassionate. The books about America this mind found interesting must be either apocalyptic or deeply ambiguous.

That manifesto came out in 1930, and went relatively unnoticed; the Southern Agrarians were just another group of experimenters in the manner of the 'twenties. Throughout the 'thirties they continued to be dismissed as reactionary in the simple sense. But during the next ten or fifteen years these men, and their disciples, produced a quantity of criticism with an air of precision and severity to which people were unaccustomed in literature. They claimed – and substantiated their claim – to be a kind of intellectual aristocracy, admitting only the best to their attention, consorting with only the finest minds in other countries and other disciplines, punishing severely any inadequate performances in their own. Their work gradually captured general attention, and they gave the study of literature a new dignity – as an exact study, a tough discipline, with high, immitigable, objectively substantial, standards. By the enthusiasm of their disciples, and by means of the text-books and anthologies they compiled for college use, this conception of literary work spread across America, and by 1950 dominated the country.

Meanwhile, they were nearly all creative as well as critical writers, and were producing poems, stories, and novels of their own. Their fiction, combined with that of writers to some degree under their inspiration, constituted what has been called the Southern Gothic school: Carson McCullers, Truman Capote, Eudora Welty, Flannery O'Connor; above all, William Faulkner. It was through this fiction rather than in their essays that the New Critics published their sense of what American literature should be and should not be. It should be elusive, allusive, symbolic, in its manner; violent and lyrical and enigmatic in its effects. It should *not* create characters or *milieux* in an importantly realistic way, and it should not evoke hearty responses to its versions of modern American life. In this indirect sense, their theory of American literature was in harmony with that of the three interpretative books; but their direct critical utterance remained quite opposite in character; they were in fact *un*sympathetic to those books. When, for instance, Allen Tate wrote about

Poe, he only alluded to D. H. Lawrence's essay, and seemed to have only half-read it; and though the New Critics' taste approved the authors who excited Lawrence – Hawthorne, Melville, Poe – and though they too made comments on American life in essays on those authors, their tone forbade the drawing of parallels. They spoke as either critics or men of letters; the difference between the two was made clear; they definitely did not speak as inspired prophets. And they became the absolute rulers of the intellectual scene; by 1950 literature in America was a single-party system; it was suffering from a sense of tyranny, of monotony, of exhaustion – but at the same time of frustrated energy. The richest veins had been worked out; but at the same time there was a plethora, a mounting apoplexy, of critical enthusiasm and ambition. Consciously and unconsciously, people wanted new modes of expression, critical and creative.

This state of affairs obtained quite generally in literary studies and literary composition; it did not apply particularly to the subject of American literature. But it was in that subject that this frustration and tension were finally resolved, and literary study began its new and exciting (and dangerous) career. That career bears the marks of a reaction against previous constraint, and we must remind ourselves of the general literary tone of the 'fifties, in order to understand it.

The feeling of frustration, imprisonment, defeat, becomes vivid as soon as we sample, however randomly, the criticism of that time. Not only the work of the New Critics themselves, but that of uncommitted commentators on literature too, those who looked at the 'party' from outside, and analysed the frustration it was causing. Some, even, were attached to other, less successful schools, like that of 'socialist realism'; who yet represented in themselves, it was clear, no way out, not even detachment, but further profitless entanglement. For their analysis of the situation not only repeated old diagnoses, it thereby made the disease seem incurable. This repetition of old truths (for instance, that of the atomisation of modern culture) not only deepened some kinds of inertia, it directed other kinds of attention and effort to the wrong projects. Some of these ideas obviously had to be sacrificed; but some had to be preserved, because the identity of the movement – whose pride was still high – depended on them. Which were sacrificed and which were preserved determined the character of the new movement.

Let us examine a few books of that time which discuss contemporary and recent American literature. Frederick J. Hoffman, in *The Twenties* (1955), devises a method of historical analysis which hinges on a New Critical-style close reading of representative texts. For each aspect of the period he finds a poem or novel, and examines it in terms first of form, then of moral and social ideas, and then of the artist's vision. Form is the most important, because literature does not report, but creates; 'the form *is* the matter, the matter is *in* the form, and the reality which is thus formally given is a moral and aesthetic anecdote of the time'. (Leslie Fiedler, in his social studies in *An End to Innocence*, tried to give to documents like the Rosenberg letters 'the same careful scrutiny we have learned to practice on the shorter poems of John Donne'.) And in the summing-up, 'Some Perspectives on the 1920s', Mr Hoffman goes through remarks on the decade by the Marxists, the liberals, the *Saturday Review of Literature*, Bernard de Voto, Van Wyck Brooks, and others, and concludes: 'None of these critics showed respect for the values of literature, only a persistent attempt to command and direct the perceptions of literary artists

in terms of an "extra-literary" set of moral imperatives.'
Here we recognise the pride with which literary studies
had been inspired by the New Critics; but we also discover how sterile that pride had become in the 'fifties.
For the most intelligent attitude we can take up to the
'twenties and to ourselves, we are told, is 'to accept the
saving grace of an irony directed at both'. The author
even offers us a formula for this irony; in the shape of a
poem by Allen Tate. Irony, scepticism and scholarship
are the qualities of modern literature. 'The writers of
the 1920s believed in everything, those of the 1930s
believed in only one thing, those of the 1940s in
nothing.' Today is the age of the scholar but not of the
creative artist. And this opposition to the artist gives
the category scholar quite Alexandrian connotations.
There is nothing creative about this scholarship.

John W. Aldridge's *After the Lost Generation* (1952)
is a survey of the fiction of the time. He finds it very
poor; and this is because the writers have found life
basically purposeless; and since they share nothing
with their audience, since there is no tradition, no
culture to give writers and readers values – or even
symbols – in common, they cannot even express that
purposelessness. We, Mr Aldridge's contemporaries,
are much more skilful, much more sophisticated, than
the writers of the 'twenties, but beside them we are
impotent. It is to the 'twenties we must go back for
inspiration. The 'thirties and its problems 'might as
well never have existed'; no one wants to hear about
the sweaty struggles of the young Studs Lonigan. (Mr
Hoffman also dismisses the 'thirties.) But we can never
equal the writers of the 'twenties, because our writers
have never known the stable society and the innocence,
the childhood experience of which gave Fitzgerald and
Hemingway the strength to denounce the adult world
they inherited. Modern culture has now reached that

stage in the process of atomisation at which it is no longer possible to communicate. For a literature you need 'the existence of a society based on certain stable moral assumptions, the sort of society to which, perhaps, Richardson and Smollett belonged, to which, in a different way and to a lesser extent, even Scott Fitzgerald and Ernest Hemingway belonged, but to which we obviously do not belong today'. This is the loudest expression of the exhaustion we are discussing, and it seems outrageous to us; but that is partly because the ten intervening years have brought such a change in the climate of opinion.

Malcolm Cowley's *The Literary Situation* (1954), discusses the New Critics and their hegemony at length and critically. Mr Cowley tells us how to recognise from an unpublished novel's folder whether it is 'new-fictional'; and how to deduce its main literary features from that category. It will be non-social, non-political, non-historical, non-intellectual; its values will be aesthetic – moral, of course, but in a way that cannot be confused with any 'extra-literary' moral imperatives; it will make great use of point-of-view, irony, ambiguity, levels of meaning, symbols, myths. And the novels that are not 'new-fictional' stand even less chance of being really original or serious. (Mr Aldridge also treated the writers who had not learned from the New Critics with even less respect than those who had.) This is because our period is 'the new age of the rhetoricians'; because the critics have established a dictatorship; poets and novelists wilt in their shadow.

All this is described in a tone of detachment, and of concern for the harm being done. But when we come to Mr Cowley's positive enthusiasm, it is for Faulkner; and that enthusiasm renewed his allegiance to the gods he claimed to question. For Faulkner (at least, as Mr Cowley read him) *was* the New Criticism, as much as

John Crowe Ransom himself. He was its living justification – the example of all its precepts and the one overwhelming proof that they worked. The critics themselves had been distinguished, but slight, creatively, and had excelled in poetry, not fiction. Faulkner, like some symbolic mountain, rose in the centre of the literary horizon, and carried the sky on his shoulders. He was obscure, he was violent, his stories were distorted into myths; he created a private world of a particular locality and particular families, just as they recommended, a world of curses and inheritances and traditions. His vision of American life was of the kind they had told us to expect from the true artist. He used the complex of social relations around him, history, climate, economic structure, even speech rhythms, merely as raw material to make a poetic world adequate to the enactment of his dramas, which were concerned with a universal and timeless pride and guilt; a world at once familiar and strange, recognisable and incredible, like a genuine myth world. Social and psychological realism counted for nothing; his characters were merely agents of his drama; and that drama was socially apocalyptic. Thus an enthusiasm for Faulkner meant an acknowledgement that the New Critics' prescriptions were after all right, and Mr Cowley's tour of the literary scene led his readers back to the point they started from.

Last of all, let us take Leslie Fiedler's *An End to Innocence* (1955), perhaps the most vivid example of the way the New Critics overlaid nascent alternatives. For in the half devoted to social studies, the author is the complete liberal, talking to liberals; but when he comes to literature we find the same vocabulary, criteria, assumptions, techniques, as in the other critics; though this vocabulary, criteria, and so on, were invented by and for a kind of conservative mind quite alien to his.

And we also find that, consequently, he can offer us no new modes or models. The modern novelist must go back to Henry James, he says; the 'thirties have nothing to offer – 'the record of the so-called proletarian novel is one of the most absurd episodes in our literary history'. His theme the young novelist is likely to derive from Melville; because Melville dealt with the ambiguity of innocence, and the mystery of iniquity; and this is the theme of the deepest American mind always. And once again the great inspiration for this beginning writer must be Faulkner.

Mr Fiedler does describe a group of writers with some independence from the New Critics; Lionel Trilling, Delmore Schwartz, Mary McCarthy, Saul Bellow and others, intellectually and politically mature in a way the New Critics are not, inhabiting the world of *Partisan Review*. They belong to the metropolitan cities; their sympathies are generally left-wing; they inherit that idealistic eloquence about America which has been reborn in this century among intellectuals from newly immigrant families, and above all among New York Jews. It is obvious that this group holds Mr Fiedler's sympathies, but it does not emerge, in this account, as essentially different in its literary orientation; 'they share the fondness of the Southern group for James and Faulkner'. Nor is his own analysis of the cultural impasse different enough to offer a way out. Both groups are starved and unable to grow, he tells us, because there is no 'gentle reader' in America, no morality to be relied on, in the reader, beyond that derived from sentimentality. Perhaps, he concludes, there can be no mature literature without a continuing tradition in the European sense; which America does not and cannot have. That verb 'cannot' may serve as our final reminder of this mood of dull despair over the whole literary enterprise in modern times.

The mood which has replaced it is not of course its opposite in every sense. Its statements about modern literature are likely to show a continuation, if not a deepening, of the same pessimism. But the tone of those statements has altered. The note of frustration and exhaustion has been replaced by something like its opposite; just as some of the leading ideas and authoritative names (though by no means all) have been changed.

The foregoing sampling was sufficient to demonstrate the effects of the decay of the New Criticism on the whole subject of literature in America. The poverty of creative work; the uniformity of critical ideas; the impotence of the opposition; the crudity of those critical ideas in their late applications; above all, the feeling of frustration, of conscious impotence, of ambitions and energies dammed up and dissipated. What was desperately needed was a new way to talk about literature, a new way to look at it, that would make it possible to discover new truths there. A need so desperate and so conscious will always find an answer, and there were hints, in the books we examined, hints readable after the event, of how literature *would* escape from this impasse.

For during the last few years a body of criticism has been appearing in America, predominantly criticism of American literature, which has a new vitality. It is partly the work of New York critics attached to the school Mr Fiedler described, and one of the sources of its new energy is that idealistic eloquence about America those left-wing writers often commanded. You found that in, for instance, Alfred Kazin's *On Native Grounds*, in 1942; the last section of which was entitled 'America! America!' and which addressed the whole country 'from Portland to Portland, from Detroit to the

Gulf, from New York to Hollywood'. You find that eloquence again in Mr Kazin's more recent work: but transmuted now to give a quite different effect; the author's interest is now less explicitly political, social, and historical; those interests are just as passionate, still, but they are all implicit in the comments on, the interpretations of, literary texts. It is a kind of inversion of Mr Hoffman's earlier attempt to extend New Critical methods. Mr Hoffman tried to write history by analysing literature; Mr Kazin, and other critics, now write criticism by analysing historical trends. That is one of the characteristics of this new critical style. The critics are discussing America through their evaluation of her literature.

But another practitioner of this style is Marius Bewley, whose primary intellectual debt is quite different; it is to F. R. Leavis, and through him to D. H. Lawrence. And the influence of *Studies in Classic American Literature* is another feature that distinguishes this new school from everything before. *On Native Grounds*, for instance, did not take Lawrence's book very seriously; but in Bewley's books, and in Richard Chase's *The American Novel and its Tradition*, its influence is primary. One of the signs is the attention devoted to James Fenimore Cooper in these books. Van Wyck Brooks and Constance Rourke are less often quoted than Lawrence, but it is the spirit of their books, too, their scope of reference, their freedom of tone, their enterprise in interpretation, which the new school imitates.

We realise the arrival of a new school most vividly of all when we turn from Leslie Fiedler's *An End to Innocence* of 1955 to his *Love and Death in the American Novel* of five years later. The enormous size of the new book is significant in itself. We see the release from New Critical constraints; the range of interests now expressed in literary interpretation; the intellectual self-confidence and enthusiasm; and we note that the author found for the first time in D. H. Lawrence's criticism, 'the kind of explication which does not betray the complexity or perilousness of its theme'. Mr Fiedler has reacted sharply away from the severities of close reading, and of purely formal appreciation; on the other hand he has inherited the high ambitions and radical vision of the New Critics. The result is a kind of hypertrophy of their interpretative method, and a series of readings which owe as much to the critic's creative imagination as to the author's. He has found a new and exciting way to talk about literature; like Mr Kazin, he has managed to include in his discussions of literature the social interests he earlier kept separate; but this new way is not criticism.

A good place to study this development is among the essays of *Interpretations of American Literature*, a critical anthology brought out in 1959 by Charles Feidelson, Jr, and Paul Brodtkorb. These essays are not chosen to represent any particular school of criticism, and as you compare their dates it is easy to see the change coming over the authors – the more political scope, the more urgent manner, the surge of new energy. It is neatly illustrated by two essays on Faulkner, Alfred Kazin on 'The Stillness of *Light in August*', and R. W. B. Lewis on 'The Hero in the New World; William Faulkner's *The Bear*'. Mr Lewis, a critic of the old school, is concerned with the timeless formal patterns of sin and redemption, with Ike McCaslin as a kind of Christ-figure, with comparisons to Homer and Virgil; Mr Kazin, in the new mode, is concerned with contemporary forces in the American psyche, with the American loneliness and the 'just-leashed violence of American life', and with comparisons to Camus and Sartre. A way has been found to turn Faulkner into a new author, to say something new and vivid about him. Criticism has escaped from the thrall of the past without having to jettison its treasures.

A beginning reader would however be startled by one feature common to both these contrasting essays; the intellectual prestige and exotic variety of the ideas invoked for the explication of a novel. This modern school is in many ways a continuation of, a development in, the New Criticism. Both groups have a strongly theoretical interest in literature; this leads in the Southern critics to a stress on form, in the New York critics to a stress on ideas; but in both the moral interest is (compared to either F. R. Leavis or Edmund Wilson) notably under the control of theory. Both have a strong political sense, of a rather apocalyptic kind, though in the New York critics this sense is closer to the normal meaning of the word politics. Both are profoundly alienated from ordinary American life, and sure that America is a uniquely difficult country for an intellectual to live in. Both are interested in the same authors; because for both the primary qualities of American literature are violence, obscurity, myth, and blasphemy. Above all, both take an enormous pride in literature, in the literary mind as a mode of intelligence.

Their differences owe something to the fact that the New York critics took their shock of inspiration from the *Second* World War; instead of the shattering of the American myth, the contact with Europe, and the right-wing reaction, they underwent the betrayal of Communism, the murder of the Jews, and the philosophy of Existentialism. Their tone involves a constant reference, more or less explicit, to the possibility of nuclear war. But the crucial difference, from our present point of view, is that they have combined with the intellectual authority of the New Critics the scope of reference of the three interpretative books. They are university teachers; they deploy upon their texts a weight of learning and technique; they bring to their judgements all the authority of an established intellectual discipline; but at the same time, by titles like *Love and Death in the American Novel*, they announce the exhilarating breadth of their interests, their refusal to be contained. They have applied their critical techniques to not just a novel or an author, but the whole of American literature, the whole of American culture, a great range of human experience. They have applied their literary sensibility to non-literary material, and the theories they formed in so doing have guided them in their critical reading.

This combination of both modes of literary comment is what gives *The American Novel and its Tradition* (to name one of the best) the intellectual glamour I spoke of. But beneath this glamour lies a combination of the weaknesses of both modes. While one never doubts Mr Chase's intelligence, or his feeling for literature, his book is not really literary criticism because it leans too heavily on truths of social prophecy, and it is not social prophecy because it deals only with questions of literary quality. It is not particular enough to be the one, and not general enough to be the other. And this is even more true of a dozen other books in the same style.

If you take for granted some large propositions about 'the American imagination', then you can of course read some remarkable (and in their way beautiful) meanings into, for instance, Tom Sawyer's adventure in the cave with Becky Thatcher. If you have an interesting theory of the American experience yourself, as most of these critics have, you can find meanings for such episodes so vivid, and, in combination with the author's simplicities, so richly odd and picturesque, that the reader is really seduced into wanting them to be valid, even if he isn't impressed into flatly believing them. But ultimately this is only a new form of the old 'creative' heresy in criticism, which used to take such forms as imaginary biographies of Shakespeare's heroines. (In fact, in discussions of *Huckleberry Finn*, Jim's deaf daughter now figures in much the same way as Lady Macbeth's children used to.) It is exciting to read, because it contains some genuine flashes of moral imagination as well as of intelligence; but it is all built on self-deception and tampering with the text.

The readings this book objects to have not all been invented during the last few years, of course. Most of them have been gaining vogue throughout the modern period, and some date even further back. But it is during the last few years that they have been elaborated and congregated and interconnected to become a body of doctrine; more important, it is during these years that this has become the basis of a general critical method. That is why it now seems worth while to speak of a new school of criticism, and to argue against those readings.

The major symptom of what is wrong, and the catastrophic result, is the attention given to Faulkner and denied to Salinger. Salinger makes practically no use of irony, ambiguity, myth, symbol, or levels of meaning. He has no violence and no obscurity. His stories take place in the 'real' world, and in a part of it as socially safe, as pictorially glamorous, as largely discursive and polite, as Henry James's (European and hypothetical) *milieux*. He portrays an America in which people are as free as Maggie Verver, to live lives as ambitious as Isabel Archer's. His fiction proceeds by richly celebrating as well as criticising that America and those ambitions. It therefore strikes most critics as not a serious imaginative effort at all. It is in the 'wrong' mode for American writing – the mode many writers begin in, but which they put behind them at the moment they reach years of discretion. He is creating life-size and lifelike characters, defined in unambiguously realistic detail, and presenting them to the reader with an affirmative enthusiasm; demanding an intimate and whole-hearted – an *unironical* – response of liking and admiration. He is insisting, among other things, on the possibility of a successful life – a life in which the individual is not dominantly conscious of damaging personal compromise. This seems categorically adolescent to those critics, who, like many American intellectuals, associate twentieth-century maturity with the emphatic disillusionment we find in Faulkner or (in more distinguished form) in T. S. Eliot. This is perhaps justifiable as a formula for maturity in America. In the life of the nation, the self-excitement of Emersonian idealism, and in the life of the individual, the self-excitement of adolescence, is something that has to be overcome by a positive effort, and with a definite shock. Americans learn with more heartbreak than other people that everything is not possible to them. Salinger's Glass family is associated with that image of themselves American intellectuals give up in the bitter moment of becoming 'mature'; the moment when they give up the dream of an eclectic and innocent brilliance which would include the most democratic use of the vernacular and the most esoteric of dead languages; when they resign themselves to the hard intellectual grind and psychological narrowing necessary to know even one subject well. According to this formula, therefore, Salinger is *categorically* immature. But no formula fits every case; in point of fact, Salinger is a hundred times more intelligent and interesting than Faulkner; moreover, every formula in time provokes the imagination to resistance; the images you can make from this idea of maturity are nowadays imaginatively dead. A novel like *Set This House on Fire* owes something to each of Faulkner and Salinger; what it owes to the latter includes by far the most living pages of the book; what it owes to Faulkner is sometimes tedious, sometimes monstrous, always imaginatively dead. And yet – and this sums up the whole predicament of American literature – the author, William Styron, proclaims his allegiance to Faulkner.

But all this is 'explanation' of 'facts' as yet unestablished. It is interesting only if important authors are in fact being quite badly misinterpreted, and if the current critical method is in fact mistaken. Those assertions it is the business of the rest of the book to substantiate; both by its own account of some major texts, and by its own more limited method. Literature of course offers insights into non-literary matters which the critic need not refuse; and adventurous reading of course demands directives from the critic's non-literary experience. There are examples of both in the essays that follow. The method is more limited in the sense that there has been at least the intention to keep those separate from the actual dealing with the text. It is the fusing or confusing of close reading with extra-literary insights which seems to me to make American literature such an unsatisfactory subject today.

Emerson:

the rejected leader

‘ Time is the little grey man who takes out of his breast-pocket
first a pocketbook, then a Dollond telescope, then a Turkey carpet, then four saddled and bridled nags and a sumptuous canvas
tent. We are accustomed to chemistry and it does not surprise us.
But chemistry is but a name for changes and developments as
wonderful as those of this Breast-Pocket.

I was a little chubby boy trundling a hoop in Chauncy Place,
and spouting poetry from Scott and Campbell at the Latin
School. But Time, the little grey man, has taken out of his vest-
pocket a great awkward house (in a corner of which I sit down
and write of him), some acres of land, several full-grown and
several very young persons, and seated them close beside me;
then he has taken that chubbiness and that hoop quite away (to
be sure he has left the declamation and the poetry), and here
left a long, lean person threatening to be a little, grey man, like
himself.   ’

Journals, Nov 11, 1842

Emerson at his best is one of the genuinely attractive
and intelligent figures in nineteenth-century American
literature. And yet he is perhaps the most disliked and
despised at the moment. Half the undergraduate papers
one reads on American literature contain scathing references to 'transcendental gush', or 'Emersonian innocence'. Critics like Yvor Winters describe him as clever,

thereby denying him both true intelligence and moral worth; indeed Winters does not scruple to use the word 'fraud'. And the scholarship about more favoured writers like Hawthorne and Melville often allows itself tones of preposterous condescension. There has been a lot of choosing of sides in American literature, and Emerson has captained the bad guys in nearly everybody's scheme for a long time. To the men of the 'twenties he symbolised everything puritan, provincial, and preachy; to those of the 'thirties, everything complacent, genteel, and bourgeois; to those of the 'forties and 'fifties, everything romantic, enthusiastic, naïve – 'he knew nothing of the dark side of human nature'. But it is not so much direct attack that has injured him as a barrage of innuendo. We may take as typical Richard Chase's remark that 'the strain of dark and somber drama which characterises so much of the best American fiction' was the work of the 'non-Emersonian' tradition of Hawthorne and Melville.

And yet the *Journals* abound in proof of a keen and beautiful intelligence. Take, for instance,

‘ How much self-reliance it implies to write a true description of anything, for example, Wordsworth's picture of skating; that leaning back on your heels and stopping in mid-career. So simple a fact no common man would have trusted himself to detach as a thought. ’

This is as pure an example of the critical mind at work as you could wish; a great deal of precise thought is compressed into the phrasing of the last sentence; and the scope and reach of the first gives literary criticism its place in a larger perspective. Or take this, a more practical, shrewd, insight.

‘ Here is our dear, grand Alcott says, You shall dig in my field for a day and I will give you a dollar when it is done, and it shall not be a business transaction! It makes me sick. Whilst money is the measure *really* adopted by us all as the most convenient measure of all material values, let us not affectedly disuse the name, and mystify ourselves and others; let us not "say no, and take it". '

The point here seems obvious and easy enough – though we should remember that Emerson had more temptations than we have to agree with Alcott. But the writing of the second and third sentences (shrewdness risking shrillness) quite unmistakably expresses the impatience of a clear mind recognising its natural enemy and opposite. Or take this, in a more poetic vein.

' The sky is the daily bread of the eyes. What sculpture in these hard clouds; what expression of immense amplitude in this dotted and rippled rack, here firm and continental, there vanishing into plumes and auroral gleams. No crowding; boundless, cheerful, and strong. '

There is a concentration of sheer thinking here too; not only in a phrase like 'daily bread of the eyes', or the incipient moralising of the last sentence, but in words like 'dotted' and 'rippled'. You feel a mind at work all the time.

Emerson was one of the most appreciative men who ever lived. He could discover what there was to like and admire in everyone he met, however different from or hostile to himself. Daniel Webster, Margaret Fuller, Monckton Milnes, Rachel, Carlyle, Hawthorne; and, through books, Napoleon, Rabelais, Montaigne, Goethe, Franklin; he had a genuine *enthusiasm* for all of them – not to mention the obvious cases like Thoreau and Alcott, Plato and Milton.

Nor was this mere facility and complaisance. No one was sharper in his criticism of even favourites like Alcott. Because of his alternation of praise and criticism, he has been more plausibly accused of inconsistency; but this is mostly a question of his manner. Emerson loved to praise, and wanted to be enthusiastic; he was distressed by his own 'cold' and 'critical' tendencies; so he stretched one-half of his response, and compressed the other, till the two seemed to have little to do with each other.

This is most true, and most off-putting, in the *Essays*; which were composed of sentences and phrases from the *Journals*, separated, repolished, and intensified. Their feeling is thus simplistic and exaggerated. It is true to some extent when you read even *extracts* from the *Journals*. For instance, Bliss Perry's selection, 'The Heart of Emerson's *Journals*', gives us this entry for 28th September 1826:

'I was born cold. My bodily habit is cold. I shiver in and out; don't heat to the good purposes called enthusiasm a quarter so quick and kindly as my neighbours.'

But if we go back to the ten-volume edition of the *Journals* we find this followed by: 'Yet, so depraved is self-conceit, that I sometimes imagined this seed of wrath to be one of my gifts, though not graces.' Which transforms the statement into something much more balanced and interesting, much more complex in tone. In fact, we discover that it was first written in a letter to his Aunt Mary, and, judging by its preceding sentence, is in answer to some external query or criticism. 'Next it seems I am cold, and when shall I kindle.' All this context not only explains the statement, it makes it more interesting, more intelligent, more impressive; and this is generally true of Emerson.

But since the *Journals* themselves were a semi-public document, the process of separation and polishing and intensification – the destruction of natural function – has been at work on even the entries there. One would like to see some of the first drafts Emerson must have thrown away. But it is quite clear without them that his was a remarkably complex and self-conflicting mind. *His* opinions really were full of tensions and rich ambiguities; it is ironic that he should be almost the only figure in American literature who has been denied these virtues by contemporary criticism.

He certainly exemplifies them better than Hawthorne and Melville, who are so much more often credited with them. By comparison with him, neither of them was an intellectual at all – really *had* opinions – and their criticisms of his 'case', now quoted at us so seriously, are little more than irritable jibes. Melville attributed Emerson's 'errors' to 'a self-conceit so intensely intellectual and calm that at first one hesitates to call it by its right name'. This could not be further off its mark; Emerson, as all the evidence shows, was one of the most painfully self-doubtful men who ever lived; his errors, like his successes, all derived from that self-doubt, that self-dislike. On another occasion, when Emerson had let himself go in print in a flight of intellectual scorn – '. . . the masses! the calamity is the masses; I do not wish any shovel-handed, narrow-brained, gin-drinking masses at all' – Melville was shocked, and invoked the Sermon on the Mount in contrast in the margin of the book. This is surely ironic when you reflect on Melville's enthusiasm for the great blasphemers, the great figures of intellectual pride, like Ahab. When he came across a real example of intellectual pride his reaction was purely parochial. Or when you reflect on the general assumption that it was Melville who dealt in the harsh realities of life, Emerson in the bland illusions. But so strong is the anti-Emersonian cast of modern criticism that Matthiessen's comment on this episode is that it shows how much more Melville knew about common life than Emerson.

As for Hawthorne, you need only compare the journals of the two men, when in Rome or London, to discover which had some real liveliness of mind, which saw and understood and discriminated, which could have 'seen through' the other. Or compare Hawthorne's mystification about the Minister's Black Veil with Emerson's 'suspicious silver veil'; where not only the image but the idea and the feeling, the subject matter, are strikingly similar.

The whole of Emerson's passage deserved to be read (it occurs in his self-examination at twenty on deciding to enter the Church) but here is half of the paragraph leading up to the reference:

‘ A score of words and deeds issue from me daily, of which I am not the master. They are begotten of weakness and born of shame. I cannot assume the elevation I ought – but lose the influence I should exert among those of meaner or younger understanding, for want of sufficient *bottom* in my nature, for want of that confidence of manner which springs from an erect mind which is without fear and without reproach. In my frequent humiliation, even before women and children, I am compelled to remember the poor boy who cried, "I told you, Father, they would find me out". Even those feelings which are counted noble and generous take in me the taint of frailty. For my strong propensity to friendship, instead of working out its manly ends, degenerates to a fondness for particular casts of feature, perchance not unlike the doting of old King James. Stateliness and silence hang very like Mokannah's suspicious silver veil, only concealing what is best not shown. What is called a warm heart, I have not. ’

The thematic material is the same as Hawthorne's, but how much sharper the analysis is, how much stronger the feeling of natural injustice and its mystery, to say nothing of the intelligence and love of truth, in Emerson's account. Or compare his portraits of Margaret

Fuller with the figure of Zenobia in Hawthorne's *Blithedale Romance*. Which of the two writers is intelligent and interesting? Which does one want to listen to?

One cannot claim much for his Transcendentalism; Emerson was no philosopher. One can only ask that it be read for what it is, a literary phenomenon. In some of his *Essays* Emerson tried to treat philosophical ideas in and for themselves; and of course he was genuinely interested in ideas; but he had no originative or instructive talent for abstract thinking. He used philosophy the way so many literary people use it: to give a form and shape to his moods, to link together his insights, as a scaffolding for his eloquence, above all as a part of his battle with his own temperament. The things he proclaimed as signally true were things he needed to convince himself of. 'We love to paint those qualities which we do not possess . . . I, who suffer from excess of sympathy, proclaim always the merits of self-reliance.' His stress on 'the infinitude of the private man' derived from his strong temptation to find himself inconsiderable, meagre, contemptible. The blatant egotism of his moral philosophy is to be explained by self-descriptions like: 'He never assumed equality with strangers, but still esteemed them older than himself, though they were of his own age or younger.' This struggle with his own personality is at the centre of his whole career. In his self-examination at 21 he writes: 'I shall not hastily conclude my soul ignobly born and its horoscope fully cast.' And at 38: 'Everybody, old men, young women, boys, play the doctor with me and prescribe for me. They always did so.' The doctrine of self-reliance is only one side of Emerson's page; the reverse contains:

'The self-subsistent shakes like a reed before a sneering paragraph in the newspaper, or even at a difference of opinion, concerning

41

something to be done, expressed in a private letter from just such another shaking bullrush as himself. He sits expecting a dinner guest with a suspense which paralyses his inventive or his acquiring faculties. He finds the solitude of two or three entire days, when mother, wife and child are gone, tedious and dispirit-ing. Let him not wrong the truth and his own experience by too stiffly standing on the cold and proud doctrine of self-sufficiency. '

It was thus against recurrent, and submerging, surges of self-contempt, not against rival philosophical sys-tems, that Emerson was proclaiming and defending his truths. He himself was fully aware how he lacked 'continuity', and how weak his 'reasoning faculty' was. He knew that his strength was in the imaginative rendering of moral insights – though one could wish he had set about that rather differently. He was speaking to and for people of the same temperament as himself; and one can say in his defence that New England then seems to have been rich in such types: Transcendental-ism will always have a historical importance, just because it was effective.

However, one cannot escape the point that there was something inferior in Emerson's performance. There is an element of self-delusion in his moral exaltation, there is something silly in his logical looseness, and if he was speaking only to people with his own tempera-mental problems, then he was deluding a lot of other auditors. The effectiveness of Transcendentalism was of an inferior kind.

But one can defend Emerson's capacities – though not his performance – by asking that his philosophising be read as intellectual self-therapy. The mind behind it then shows itself as much less vague, simple, and thin. The critical formula: 'Emerson has left a handful of essays and poems which are to many an essential part of their religious literature; but the man himself evades discovery' – which occurs in the *Literary History of the United States* – is surely the reverse of the truth.

If the brash egotism of the essays is due to the writer's self-doubt, their ecstatic tone (which has often seemed another kind of egotistic irresponsibility) owes something to his dutifulness. Emerson always felt a strong call to supply the 'Age' with what it needed; and what his Age needed, he thought, plausibly enough, was large, sublime, truths. He grew up in the heyday of romanticism, and literary people were abnormally conscious of the meanness of their daily life in contrast with Byronic raptures and despairs. Moreover, the most flourishing literary tradition in America was that of inspirational oratory; and, in the persons of Daniel Webster and Edward Everett, oratory was delivering large sublime truths to the New England of Emerson's youth. He seemed peculiarly marked out for public speaking, too; both by his ministerial ancestry and by his personal endowment with a speaking voice unexpectedly powerful and noble. It was therefore natural that he should listen to these two great speakers with excitement – sometimes excluding the words, the better to concentrate on their vocal music; that he should remain fascinated with them as men all his life; that he should consciously imitate them, even in their writing style. One can see that everything in his temperament and his conscience would draw him to this self-schooling; but one has to regard it as unfortunate.

Neither Webster nor Everett had the quality of mind, or the kind of mind, that Emerson could imitate with profit. And the large sublime tone of public speaking can rarely be imported into literary discourse; it becomes blatant and vulgar there. The effects of largeness and grandeur Emerson wanted to produce can only succeed in literature when there is a poetic tradition available for the artist to use; and there was not for

Emerson. Above all, Emerson was not a large, sublime man. His strength lay partly in his weakness – in the courage, generosity and justice with which he handled that – in his steady appreciativeness and responsiveness towards all the personalities and ideas which imposed themselves on him; and partly in his fine intelligence. Only a critic like Woodberry, who found 'no friction, no disturbance, no unrest' in the *Journals*, could have called Emerson 'the only great mind America has produced in literature'. Emerson was not a 'great' man; he did not think he was; but he thought the age needed greatness, and he gave it the best he could offer in that line.

He was endowed moreover with a kind of literary equivalent of his vocal gift; the gift of phrase-making. He could give an effective turn to any group of words. And under the impulsion of his duty to the age (and also his love of the powerful mode) he produced quantities of noble-sounding phrases, and delivered them in a noble-sounding voice; and intoxicated himself as well as his audience. But we are not intoxicated. We are cloyed and irritated. His phrases are too much of a kind. We see how the trick is done; that it is, as Winters says, 'clever'. What we want from a man with this talent is what we find sometimes in the *Journals*; writing with a *variety* of tone, different *kinds* of phrases, swiftness of *transition*, so that a paragraph mirrors a succession, a shifting, of moods, all bound together by a strong intelligence and a keen moral purpose.

For instance, this, written at 18:

‘ Look next from the history of my intellect to the history of my heart. A blank, my lord. I have not the kind affections of a pigeon. Ungenerous and selfish, cautious and cold, I yet wish to be romantic; have not sufficient feeling to speak a natural, hearty welcome to a friend or stranger, and yet send abroad wishes and fancies of a friendship with a man I never knew. There is not in the whole wide Universe of God (my relations to Himself I do not understand) one being to whom I am attached with warm and entire devotion – not a being to whom I have joined fate for weal or woe, not one whose interests I have nearly and dearly at heart; – and this I say at the most susceptible age of man. Perhaps at the distance of a score of years, if I then inhabit this world, or still more, if I do not, these will appear frightful confessions; they may or may not, – it is a true picture of a barren and desolate soul. ,

The writing here is still boyish in some sense; and the tone does not vary very much; but what vivacity and energy of phrasing – what a strong impression of *life*, in counterpoint with the death-bearing statement.

This you do not find in the essays. Of course, they *are* morally and intellectually impressive in their way; one can believe that to a contemporary, to whom the ideas, the issues, the problems, would be alive – for instance, the fate of Unitarianism – they could be very exciting. One can understand why Matthew Arnold declared them the most important prose of the century; more important than Carlyle's; the equivalent of Wordsworth's poetry. For many of his contemporaries they embodied, in Arnold's words, 'the friend and aider of those who would live in the spirit'. But for us nowadays, they present only glimpses of the man who attracts and interests us. We are always being choked off with moral paradoxes and hyperboles, carved and polished and framed to a degree that deprives them of organic life, and yet not interlocked enough to make a significant system.

The man who attracts and interests us is one of the world's masters of self-doubt and self-dislike. He deserves the title because he explored the experience with clarity of mind and firmness of touch, and also with a suppleness and freedom of tone which makes him the master, not the prisoner, of its moods. At 20 he wrote:

' I have set down little which can gratify my vanity, and I must further say that every comparison of myself with my mates that six or seven, perhaps sixteen or seventeen, years have made, has convinced me that there exists a signal defect of character which neutralises in great part the just influence my talents ought to have. Whether that defect be in the *address*, in the fault of good forms, – which, Queen Isabella said, were like perpetual letters-commendatory – or deeper seated in an absence of common *sympathies*, or even in a levity of the understanding, I cannot tell. But its bitter fruits are a sore uneasiness in the company of most men and women, a frigid fear of offending and jealousy of disrespect, an inability to lead and an unwillingness to follow the current conversation, which contrive to make me second with all those among whom chiefly I wish to be first.

Hence my bearing in the world is the direct opposite of that good-humoured independence and self-esteem which should mark the gentleman. Be it here remembered that there is a decent pride which is conspicuous in the perfect model of a Christian man. I am unfortunate also, as was Rienzi, in a propensity to laugh, or rather, snicker. I am ill at ease, therefore, among men. I criticise with hardness; I lavishly applaud; I weakly argue; and I wonder with a "foolish face of praise". '

The next paragraph begins: 'Now the profession of law demands . . .', and the next: 'But in Divinity I hope to thrive . . .' All the way through his control is superb; he deals with these really corrosive truths exactly as with neutral ones, and is always ready also to praise himself, both in behaviour and talents, and highly. 'Entire success in the first [preaching] is the lot of few, but this I am encouraged to expect.' This was his own encouragement, his own faith in himself; the world at large had no great expectations of Emerson at that time. But indeed the prose itself – the coolness, the largeness, of his references to Rienzi and Queen Isabella – demonstrates that control.

The liveliest of these passages all occur in the early years of the *Journal* entries; that is perhaps why they have been so largely disregarded – as typically adolescent, and as not typically Emersonian. But I would claim that all we find most interesting in Emerson is quite radically related to them, and that they are in themselves more vivid and powerful than a category like 'adolescent' does justice to. This was the struggle, not any other, which energised and organised *all* Emerson's talents; as he relaxed from this he lost his power to excite others. In the second half of his life his serenity became blandness. This struggle is moreover the feature of his work which best places it in the larger traditions.

What Emerson suffered from was related to what made Keats feel oppressed, crowded out of himself, by the presence of another personality in the room; and equally to what made Kafka unable to escape his father's domination. This 'sensitiveness' runs through the history of Western literature since 1800 as persistently as tuberculosis. At different times the disease has been differently handled by the sufferers – sometimes exploited, sometimes concealed, sometimes explicitly denied. But there are few whose work is not affected, whose quality is not to some degree constituted, by the way they handled it. The two greatest figures, Tolstoy and D. H. Lawrence, were the two most gifted with the contrary strength – the 'animal spirits' Emerson so bitterly envied in others, for lacking which he so bitterly condemned himself – but Lawrence and Tolstoy too suffered from 'sensitiveness'. It was Lawrence's constant cry that he was being bullied; that people and ideas were trying to control and dominate and interfere with him. ('Everybody, old men, young women, boys, all

47

play the doctor with me and prescribe for me. They always did so.') Lawrence's doctrine of the blood as much as Emerson's of self-reliance needs to be understood in that context.

Indeed, Emerson reminds us of Lawrence in many of his ways of combining moral severity with personal autonomy. They were two of the world's great Protestants. Both started from, and always took for granted, a puritanical Christian moral training. Both were very interested in, ambitious of, personal and social force. Both resisted the claims of charity and reform very fiercely. 'The worst of charity', said Emerson, 'is that the lives you are asked to preserve are not worth preserving.' Both were aristocratic by intellectual temperament, though in no political or social sense. In moral and spiritual matters, both were concerned for *health* above everything; Emerson was in reaction against Byronism as well as Calvinism, Lawrence against aestheticism as well as orthodox moralism.

Emerson was however not a genius. His solution to the problem of 'sensitiveness' was, compared with Lawrence's, a compromise. It was midway between the latter's achievement of strength and Kafka's embracement of weakness. It was the kind of noble compromise we associate with the names of Turgenev, Forster, and Trilling; the weakness is accepted; buttressed with a variety of skills and interests, intellectual, social, aesthetic; with a beautifully clear, broad, tolerant, appreciative mind; but without attempting to disguise or cancel the one with the others. Men of this kind have been the conscience of the Western world. They are particularly associated with the cause of liberalism in all its phases. They represent one of the triumphs of Western civilisation, in its more passive mode. Though, because they have so frankly enacted weakness, they have had more than their share of humiliating patronage from the literary world. Thus one ('sympathetic') critic* feels free to say – of an incident in Emerson's first marriage –

> ❛ Any woman who is a true female (which does not always follow) will have the man, or men, of her choice unconditionally. Emerson is also true to type, not that of the true male, but that of the philosopher, who praises life in the raw but prefers it cooked. ❜

Men like Emerson bring out the brawny male in every twopenny essayist and penny newspaper columnist. They have assumed and lived out everyone's weakness.

We have given examples enough of the variety of Emerson's interests. What needs to be added, to justify aligning him with men like Turgenev and Forster, is that he could make a unity out of them, that he could – surely the crucial test of a distinguished literary mind – combine intellectual, moral, and aesthetic criteria harmoniously in a single judgement. Thus he wrote about his brother Charles: 'His elegance, his wit, his sense, his worship of principle, I shall not find united – I shall not find them separate.' And all his remarks on the influence of wealth on character; on Southern personality types versus Northern; on the Englishman versus the American; on the revelatory power of the eyes (in 'Behaviour'); all these are the work of a gifted observer, a great connoisseur, of manners; that subject in which the combination of different criteria, their interpenetration and mutual adjustment, is uniquely necessary.

One can contrast him here with Thoreau, who had a much stiffer and narrower mind. It is true, as is often said, that Thoreau lived by his principles, whereas Emerson only talked about his; and that *Walden* is a

*Holbrook Jackson, in *Dreamers of Dreams*.

more logical result and natural product of Transcendentalism than anything of Emerson's. It is true that Thoreau escaped the debilitating shame and guilt that wasted so much of Emerson's energy. But Emerson was larger than his principles; he saw and heard and knew a great deal that didn't fit them. And if Thoreau secured himself against weakness, he secured himself also against understanding. He achieved himself – achieved an integrity and firmness of character Emerson never did – but he did so by refusing (at pre-conscious levels, of course) to know what would have disturbed that firmness; Emerson did all his refusing at the conscious levels – *unconsciously*, everything and everyone imposed themselves on him, and his only revenge was to understand and judge them. Thoreau solved his problems successfully but, as so often, the problem was more interesting than the solution. It is Emerson who means more to us; his defeats were a greater triumph for humane intelligence.

There is always a sadness, a disappointment, about the performance of the class of minds I have put Emerson in. We feel they could have done more. This is perhaps even more marked with Emerson, however, than with the others. He didn't manage to make anything out of his wealth of insights. He was very conscious of this failure. 'If Minerva offered me a gift and an option,' he wrote at 50, 'I would say "give me continuity". I am tired of scraps. I do not wish to be a literary or intellectual chiffonier. Away with this Jew's rag-bag of ends and tufts of brocade, velvet, and cloth-of-gold; let me spin some yards or miles of helpful twine, a clew to lead to one kingly truth, a cord to bind wholesome and belonging facts.' The idea of a 'kingly' truth is what led him astray before; the best he could do in that line he had already done; it was what was now dissatisfying him. His essays are, we may say, the cloth-of-gold tufts pasted end to end on paper. But what kind of continuity *could* have been his? What kind of wholesome and belonging facts *could* he have bound together? We find a clue in the work of the three men I have aligned him with. Consider these two comments of his on Margaret Fuller:

> Margaret is "a being of unsettled rank in the universe". So proud and presumptuous, yet so meek; so worldly and artificial and with keenest sense and taste for all pleasures of luxurious society, yet living more than any other for long periods in a trance of religious sentiment; a person who, according to her own account of herself, expects everything for herself from the Universe . . . Some persons are thrown off their balance when in society; others are thrown on to balance; the excitement of company and the observation of other characters correct their biases. Margaret Fuller always appeared to unexpected advantage in conversation with a circle of persons, with more common sense and sanity than any other, – though her habitual vision was through coloured lenses.

Surely it is a novelist's sensibility we recognise here. Not that we think of Hawthorne's Zenobia; it is a much more interesting person described and describing; but we can think of George Eliot's Maggie. Emerson had the same interests as George Eliot; what he saw in Coleridge, in Thoreau, in Alcott, in Webster, in Miss Emerson, is what she would have seen, the class of facts she did see in Mr Casaubon, Adam Bede, Gwendolen Harleth, Lydgate. He had also a similar power of moralising metaphor, of abstract generality made vivid by concrete image. What his portraits lack is detail; detail of characterisation, of social *milieu*, of how events happen; these are the wholesome and belonging facts he needed to achieve continuity. But he was bewitched by his 'duty' to produce kingly truths for the age.

But Emerson is still more attractive to us than this description accounts for. He is a hero of weakness; a fine humanist; a novelist *manqué*; but he is something more. He represents America to us – he is the profile of that America which has meant so much to me, for one – and the current fashion of denying him in favour of, for instance, a Faulknerian Gothic America, seems to me a form of self-destruction.

Emerson represents America to us first because we find in him so many of those attitudes which in Americans strike a European as so typical of the country. Take for instance his reaction to hearing that 'a young girl in the midst of rich, decorous Unitarian friends in Boston' was to join the Roman Catholic Church:

> ' But I told them that I think she is to be greatly congratulated on the event. She has lived in great poverty of events. In form and years a woman, she is still a child, having had no experiences,* and although of a fine, liberal, susceptible, expanding nature, has never yet found any worthy object of attention; has not been in love . . .   '

This tone always seems to a European faintly comical – such public discussion of such private matters; and faintly disturbing – such a measuring outwards, from the individual's needs to his religious allegiance. They seem comical and disturbing to sophisticated Americans equally, but the latter are the first to describe them as an American phenomenon. Another such symptom, in education, is the demand that a subject 'satisfy', in some immediate sense; that classes follow and form some natural rhythm in the student's inner life. It is in Emerson we find the classical statements of all such ideas; for instance, the advice to close the book the moment it has begun to suggest to you your own

*Emerson praised Margaret Fuller for her 'large experiences': and his use of the word is usually very modern.

thoughts on its topic. Emerson is the classical voice of a curious American 'existentialism'; in which the present moment is the measure of all things, and the individual *must* always ask himself how much he is feeling at the moment.

‘ I have no expectation that any man will read history aright, who thinks that what was done in a remote age, by men whose names have resounded far, has any deeper sense than what he is doing today. ’

This existentialism subordinates everything to its moral aspect, with an effect that can seem sometimes amoral. In education, for instance, one's intellectual work is only an episode in one's total life-adventure; it must be always subordinate to that. Better than any industrious collegian is the sturdy lad who 'teams, farms, peddles, keeps school, edits'; because he 'does not postpone his life but lives it'.

It is true that if Emerson supremely represented only *these* aspects of the American temperament, the point would be ambiguous; for they are not the finest aspects. It is clear how much laziness, fancifulness, and intellectual egotism such ideas can and do foster. Though one should remember that in their less obtrusive forms, when so blended with seriousness and hard work as to lose their sharp edges, they become great sources of intellectual energy.

But the spirit of Emerson is also, and more importantly, incarnated in a great American institution, which is a training ground, if not a career and a way of life, for a large section of her literary intellectuals. Freshman English, English Composition I, the compulsory course for all college freshmen, is a training in how to write, but also, quite importantly, in how to think. It is an educational course in the broadest sense.

The students are called upon to have opinions, on large general issues; to have reasons for their opinions; to accept or reject other opinions, reasonably. They must read essays that confront them with judgements, ideas, experiences, which challenge their assumptions. But it is taught by people getting, or just having got, their Ph.Ds in English. It is therefore a very literary idea of general education and the intellectual life which it realises. It deals with thought in the forms in which language, sophisticated literary language, embodies it.

Whatever the effect on the students, such a course has a profound effect on the instructors. This is their first teaching, and it is of an unusually demanding kind; they are facing a cross-section of American society, not so much younger than themselves, and representing to them the intellectual's approach to general topics. They are justifying themselves. The way in which they do it is therefore of the first importance. The impress of this experience transfers itself – though less vividly – to other parts of American literary life.

The inspiration behind such teaching when it is well done is a kind of Transcendentalism; for Transcendentalism was really a literary movement with a moral and educational ambition; it was groups of people discussing ideas in literature for the moral and educational value of the exercise – trying to bring to bear on their daily life the inspiration of literature, and on their reading the realism of practical life; to integrate and interfuse a man's whole experience through the medium of his language; and this -- in its most high-flown formulation -- is just what Freshman English aims at. It encompasses all other branches of knowledge and experience through literature; not literature in the sense of aesthetic forms so much as in the sense of meaningful language – language being used to create as well as convey meaning – language embodying and enacting significant attitudes. This is what Emerson meant by literature. Carlyle, even in his histories and his philosophising, was for Emerson a *literary* figure; and, just because of the scope he gave to the word 'literary', he was also the supreme Transcendentalist.

Thus used, 'literary' obviously covers a great deal of intellectual life; but it also omits or distorts a great deal. We can see the likeness between Transcendentalism and its modern descendant also in what they both distort. Thus Emerson says: 'We shall learn one day to supersede politics by education', and he does not wait for that day. As for history and sociology: 'An institution is the lengthened shadow of one man', and 'Society never advances. For everything that is given, something is taken.' And science means only the mechanical application of limited logical faculties. Such fallacies always threaten to blight 'literary' versions of general education. But the queer blend of moral enthusiasm, intellectual rigour, and emotional caution, which characterises Freshman English, is Emerson's more than anybody else's. Intellectual plain living and high thinking is its motto; most forms of sophistication are deprecated – because, in such students, they are usually ways of evading the issue. The moral life is all within you, in your own use of language; what is outside, in the form of exact knowledge, or social action, is secondary; stay at home and think great thoughts. This is quintessential Emerson. In Trilling's beautiful story about Freshman English, 'Of This Time, Of That Place', he gives the central character an essay-style like that of Emerson's *Journals*; and when Emerson sums up other people's analyses of the contemporary scene: 'To me, however, the question of the times resolved itself in a practical question of the conduct of life. How shall I live?' we catch the deepest intonation, the ultimate aspiration, of this kind of teaching. Training in this institution makes the spirit of Emerson live on in modern America, and gives many of her intellectuals – even those with categorically sophisticated tastes – an incongruous Emersonian cast.

However, though an Englishman will find this strange, he will also find it familiar, if he has had a literary training. For Emerson's idea of literature as a great moral discipline, as *the* great modern discipline, is one he shared with the best nineteenth-century English minds, like Arnold and Carlyle. 'Literature is but a branch of Religion', said the latter, 'and always participates in its character; however, in our times, it is the only branch that still shows any greenness; and, as some think, must one day become the main stem.' This tradition has disappeared in England more than once, and has changed its externals very thoroughly; but it is still with us, and finding its best flowering, today, in the critical work of F. R. Leavis, the creative work of D. H. Lawrence, and the educational influence of them and their disciples. This is an English tradition which has a lot in common with the New England one; literary sensibility and literary discrimination become in both the agents of moral, indeed religious, passions. That is why Emerson can remind us of Lawrence (as distinct from, say, Forster, whom in other ways he much more resembles); because he remained a Puritan while he became a humanist; because his kind of Transcendentalism, at its most rigorous, is one of the inspirations of our great modern literary movement. And that is why Freshman English can be to an Englishman not only a discovery of the best in America, but a rediscovery of the best in England. They, the course and the man, give us a sense of the relationship between the two countries.

Emerson said: 'England tends to accumulate her liberals in America and her conservatives at London,'

– thinking of intellectual temperament as expressed in literary rather than political opinions. He claimed that the idealistic, intellectual, and poetic strains in the British heritage found freer play in America, that in nineteenth-century England the imagination moved in a thicker atmosphere, encumbered as well as enriched by circumstance, tradition, and 'worldliness'. This is a plausible enough view, and, as so often with Emerson, not so single-valued as it sounds; compare Emerson himself with George Eliot, Hawthorne with Thackeray, Lowell with Arnold, and the advantage obviously lies with the thicker atmosphere.

It was also a very popular view at the time. In the *Biglow Papers* Lowell wrote:

'Yet, after all, thin speculative Jonathan is more like the Englishman of two centuries ago than John Bull himself is. He has lost somewhat in solidity, has become fluent and adaptable, but more of the original groundwork of character remains. He feels more at home with Fulke Greville, Herbert of Cherbury, Quarles, George Herbert and Browne, than with his modern English cousins. He is nearer than John, by at least a hundred years, to Naseby, Marston Moor, Worcester, and the time when, if ever, there were true Englishmen. John Bull has suffered the idea of the invisible to be very much fattened out of him. Jonathan is conscious still that he lives in the world of the Unseen as well as of the Seen. To move John you must make your fulcrum of solid beef and pudding; an abstract idea will do for Jonathan. '

And if America was nearer the past than England, she was also nearer the future. The mention of seventeenth-century writers should remind us that when England rediscovered the Metaphysicals after the turn of the century, she was in a sense recovering a heritage (after a surfeit of 'beef and pudding') which literary America had never lost. America, moreover, now offered something of its own; the idealistic nonconformist mind in England then – the heritage Lawrence was born to – found Emerson and Thoreau more purely congenial prophets than almost any English writer. It is the more persuasive half of Lawrence's thesis in *Studies in Classical American Literature* that in America the liberalising and idealising phase of the European mind had been pushed to its logical extreme. In these ways America *was* ahead of England; in the way that liberals are ahead of conservatives; the contrast between the two countries followed the lines Emerson indicated.

But that contrast is today so changed as to seem almost reversed; nevertheless, Emerson still gives us the vital clue to its design. Let us notice that the American Lowell defined is a very Emersonian figure. He is far from what most people think of now as a typical American; he could scarcely have been described thus at the time, but for all Emerson had done and been. Emerson *was*, as much as any individual, the 'Jonathan' Lowell described. He could not be taken as a model of a contemporary Jonathan; but he is recognisably related to, the grandfather of, the intellectual American I found; in whom I and others rediscovered our sense of family. Other strains of heritage have influenced that American's make-up; some of them opposed in tendency; but none of equal moral strength. The same is true of the Arnoldian heritage of the literary Englishman. The literary American and his counterpart in England are related primarily through membership of different branches of the Transcendental heritage. All that is usually associated with that name they may repudiate, from time to time; they may espouse the opposite principles, to avoid a threatened imbalance; but the deepest sources of their energy remain what they were.

These truths are obscured at present by the general

acceptance of a picture of Transcendentalism, and of Emerson, which amounts to a caricature. The attack on him during the first two decades of this century was justified; there was so much to be achieved by working in a direction the opposite to that he represented; but to continue now to identify him with a number of sonorous platitudes is fruitless and stupid. Combined with the enthusiasm for Faulkner, moreover, it is radically perverse. It deforms the image of America in several ways. That enthusiasm is aroused, most typically, by Faulkner's treatment of the Negro theme; his heavy stress on the tragic inevitability of the situation, his total deprecation of 'solutions'; which is sometimes explicitly contrasted with Emerson's active abolitionism. The proof of literary sophistication is thereby equated with a hostility to social and political action of any kind – the guarantee of sensibility becomes intense inaction. The whole range of rational moral effort (represented by Freshman English, say) is dismissed as naïve, in favour of a brooding rhetoric of doom. The *real* America becomes the conflict of subterranean and savage forces; an archaic, endless, irreconcilable conflict, portrayable only in Gothic art; and the other sides of American life are epi-phenomena. But what is even more radical is the disregard this preference announces for all the manifestations of intelligence in literary work. A scheme of literary values which promotes Faulkner far above Emerson, which finds the former a far more intelligent and attractive figure, is simply grotesque.

The Hawthorne Myth:

a protest

Hawthorne's reputation remains very high in America. In the last ten years at least seven book-length studies have appeared (by authors as well known as Marius Bewley and Harry Levin) which all present him as a moulder and hero of the modern sensibility. They differ in details of their interpretation, but there is on the whole a remarkable critical unanimity about his work; as an allegorical articulation of the deepest and darkest experience of the American psyche. It is still, however, possible to take a different view, and to feel that the critics are inventing meanings for their texts; that Hawthorne's own account of his work is shrewder than theirs.

Hawthorne called his longer works of fiction romances, and his shorter ones tales or sketches, and he defined his sense of those terms.

' The sketches are not, it is hardly necessary to say, profound ... They never need translation . . . They are not the talk of a secluded man with his own mind and heart (had it been so, they could hardly have failed to be more deeply and permanently valuable) but his attempts, and very imperfectly successful ones, to open an intercourse with the world. '

This comes from Hawthorne's preface to the third

edition of *Twice-Told Tales*; a collection which includes 'Young Goodman Brown'. None of Hawthorne's critics has failed to praise his judgement of his own work; but they have all assumed such remarks to be not the modifications of modesty, but a flat contradiction of the truth. They have insisted that the sketches fall into a quite opposite category; that they are 'profound', that they always need translation, that they *are* a dialogue with his own mind and heart, and *not* a performance as clubman-author.

The Preface to *The House of the Seven Gables* begins,

'When a writer calls his work a Romance, it need hardly be observed that he wishes to claim a certain latitude, both as to its fashion and material, which he would not have felt himself entitled to assume, had he professed to be writing a Novel. '

This latitude is a freedom from the rigorous discipline of realism, and a freedom in the management of 'his atmospherical medium'; a freedom to 'bring out or mellow the lights, and deepen and enrich the shadows, of the picture'. The device he has most in mind, it appears, is 'the Marvellous'; ghosts, curses, legends, superstitions, omens, etc. The romance writer will not ask his reader to believe in these things; he will be wise, no doubt, 'to mingle the Marvellous rather as a slight, delicate, and evanescent flavor . . .' He will describe the superstition, that is, dismiss it laughingly, and then give a hint that perhaps something uncanny really did happen; and isn't it anyway rather nice to think it did. He will not ask us to believe in anything supernatural, or make it 'any portion of the actual substance of the dish offered to the public'. In all this, as he himself observes, Hawthorne is describing a genre with which the readers of 1851 were very familiar. In calling his book a romance and not a novel, he is promising them something in the manner of Mrs Radcliffe and her successors. That, moreover, is what he gave them. *The House of the Seven Gables*, *The Scarlet Letter*, *The Marble Faun*, *The Blithedale Romance*, are romances in that sense. They differ from novels just in the thinness of their psychological and sociological detail, in their fascination with the supernatural, in the liberties they take with their own verisimilitude; their essential meaning lies in the author's persona, in his comments as he conjures up before us, and then dispels, various quaint, gloomy, or charming scenes.

The critics, however, insist that Hawthorne had his own conception of the romance, quite different from Mrs Radcliffe's; that for him it was a form in which the psychological aspects of spiritual experience could be symbolically rendered. First of all, it is unlikely that *any* writer could do that without being conscious of it; without in fact saying something about it, in notebook or journal if not in conversation. This is a complex aesthetic strategy; not the sort of thing that gets done unconsciously. Hawthorne made copious notes for and about his own writing; but they contain no proof that he thought of writing anything but the tales and romances he defined in his prefaces. Secondly, Hawthorne in particular was not an intellectual writer in any sense. James remarks several times on how empty of ideas the Journals are, and there is every evidence that Hawthorne never took part in a conversation about ideas or forms in his life. He spent a lot of time in solitary meditation, but he described this as musing or dreaming, and the evidence supports him. When irritated by the intellectual enthusiasm of his Concord neighbours, Hawthorne's recourse was not to a profounder understanding of the American experience, but to the great established truths of the popular heart, Christianity, marriage, democracy.

No one, of course, can read Hawthorne without realising that there is something very different and very deep below the surface. As he makes his comments, and invokes his pieties, his voice moves into and out of disturbing echoes produced by a hollow cavity below, quite thinly iced over. But one can feel that Hawthorne gave those depths no voice of their own; that they remained only a distorting and ominous echo. In fact, though they constitute the prime interest of his work for us now, they probably spoiled it for him and his readers then; they probably prevented him from doing well the kind of writing he was aiming at.

To explain this reading of Hawthorne, it is simplest to refer directly to the facts of his life. His father died while he was a child, his mother withdrew from the world, and his sisters treated him as the most important member of the family. A very handsome, sensitive boy, much petted by them and by his aunts and uncles, and invited into solitude both by the decline of the family fortunes and by his own illness, he seems to have drifted away from normal contacts into a dreamland of stories, totally unchallenged, unaroused, knowing no equals.

At Bowdoin he cultivated the less perceptive, less challenging companions. 'He would sit for a whole evening with head gently inclined to one side, hearing every word, seeing every gesture, and yet scarcely a word would pass his lips. . . . He lives in a mysterious world of thought and imagination which he never permits me to enter.' Cilley assumed that since his friend did not live fully in the normal world of people and things, then he must live in the world of thought and imagination. But Hawthorne tells us over and over that a man may live in neither, may refuse fruitful reciprocation with any aspect of reality. And all the details of Cilley's account confirm Hawthorne's diagnosis; the silence, the watchfulness, the head on one side, the physical clumsiness, the hours of dreaming, the shyness and the lethargy.

Then came twelve appalling years at Salem. Mark van Doren may think them a period of hard work, relieved by diversions and friendships, punctuated by the excitements of artistic accomplishment. Hawthorne was appalled by them. He sat alone in his room all day and night for twelve years; he even sent his sister to the library for him, and only went out himself after dark; he read without studying, mused without thinking, and wrote fanciful, unreal, little sketches. He watched people in the street and made up stories about them, but refused to meet them socially. Such behaviour could seem, in the 1830s, typical of a writer, and even distinguished, though eccentric. But when he found that his stories were malicious, that they invaded the other person's most sacred privacy, that they were not at all as warm and kindly as, for instance, Dickens's stories, then he felt guilty and frightened. He made great efforts to come out into the world and 'open an intercourse' with people. But part of his nature resisted. Playing with imaginary characters was much easier for him than responding to real ones. All his life he spoke of 'the heart' as something that needed constant attention and encouragement, needed will-power and work behind it, not to wither and dwindle away. He was, it appears, strongly tempted to dissipate reality, and especially the reality of other people and their demands on him, by absorbing himself in stories which he did not really believe; to divert all his energy to the creation of an imaginary universe which he could dismiss at will, and which could never, therefore, achieve independent reality. He found a temporary safety from this temptation in marriage; but it seems from the history of the years after his return from

Europe that it renewed its attack on him and finally triumphed.

This is the picture that emerges from Newton Arvin's account of Hawthorne's life. It is of course somewhat simplified, and relies heavily on Hawthorne's own testimony; perhaps it overlooks the mitigating features. But it is much more convincing than any interpretation based on those mitigating features alone, as Mark van Doren's and Randall Stewart's seem to be.

The Notebooks are full of evidence that this temptation was in fact the problem that interested Hawthorne most, and most personally; that this was the experience that demanded expression in him, which he approached, backwards, so often, and which gave that disturbing echo to his cheerfully pitched voice, in, for instance, 'Wakefield'. In 1837 he wrote:

> Insincerity in a man's own heart must make all his enjoyments, all that concerns him, unreal; so that his whole life must seem like a merely dramatic representation. And this would be the case even though he were surrounded by true-hearted relatives and friends.

The precision and sombreness of his observations on this theme are far superior to anything else in the Notebooks. In 1838:

> Character of a man who, in himself and his external circumstances, shall be equally and totally false; his fortune resting on baseless credit – his patriotism assumed – his domestic affections, his honor and honesty, all a sham. His own misery in the midst of it – it making the whole universe, heaven and earth alike, an unsubstantial mockery to him.

Let us note that the insincerity and the falsity are not only in the man's relations with the outside world, but also in himself; so that everything is *unreal* to him.

These are the thoughts, the experience, we must recall when he described those years in such terms as 'dreamy', 'dreary', 'idle musings', 'the Dreamland of my youth', and 'an attempt to open an intercourse with the world'. In his letters to his wife he was always quite explicit about the unreality, the unsubstantiality, of his life before he met her. And if we remember the mid-Victorian standard of sensibility, sympathy, warm-heartedness; a standard his wife lived up to, and Hawthorne acted up to in his public persona – all the 'sweet young girls' and 'dainty little children' he invoked; then we need not wonder that this kind of guilt should have been so appalling, so unspeakable.

In his fiction, his tales and romances, this disease shows its effects most obviously in his delight in unreality. He plays on the doubtful distinction between appearance and reality, especially in the matter of the supernatural, more than any other writer. He is always pretending that something frightening or abnormal has happened (that Mistress Hibbins is literally a witch) without letting go of a safe contrasting ordinariness underneath. It appears also in his descriptions. His finest pieces of this kind, for instance that of Peter-borough Close, or the gardens of the Villa Borghese, have an extraordinarily suspended, timeless, unreal quality; the exact opposite of the quality D. H. Lawrence caught in his descriptions. And in his last piece of fiction, *Septimius Felton*, we find the same painful chord being struck as in the early years.

'Septimius went into his house, and sat in his study for some hours, in that unpleasant state of feeling which a man of brooding thought is apt to experience when the world around him is in a state of intense action, which he finds it impossible to sympathise with. There seemed to be a stream rushing past him, by which, even if he plunged into the midst of it, he could not be wet. He felt himself strangely ajar with the human race, and would have given much either to be in full accord with it, or to be separated from it forever.   "

The simplicity and vividness of the metaphor in the second sentence, and the recklessness of the last, are a guarantee that Hawthorne's imagination was excited personally by this theme.

"I am dissevered from . . . the human race . . . It is my doom to be only a spectator of life; to look on as one apart from it . . . How cold I am now, while this whirlpool of public feeling is eddying around me! It is as if I had not been born of woman.   "

So far, however, this reading of Hawthorne does not differ importantly from that of many critics who include him in the highest pantheon. Newton Arvin, for instance, thinks him a sick man but a great writer.

Hawthorne himself aimed at being a *good* writer, in the Victorian sense, with a charming, cheerful, humorous style, tolerant, bourgeois, warm-hearted, full of honest sentiment and stout common sense. He hoped his tales would pass an hour pleasantly, cause an agreeable shudder, even dampen the eye of an especially soft-hearted maiden; greatness he did not aim at.

This moreover is the Hawthorne Henry James admired. In James's comments on the Notebooks and on Hawthorne's style in general, it is the word charming that recurs more than any other. But modern readers find Hawthorne unsuccessful in this genre. All his children are little personages, all his girls snowy virgins, who trip instead of walking, all his boys honest youths, all unmarried women ancient or withered or decayed maidens. Reading Hawthorne, you never touch reality, but a thick layer of literary quilting.

"In short, to bring the matter at once to a point, it was incontrovertibly evident that somebody had taken the shop and fixtures of the long-retired and forgotten Mr Pyncheon and was about to renew the enterprise of that long-departed worthy, with a different set of customers.   '

A thick wadding of words interposes between the reader and the object; and those words have in them no freshness or tension; they come from the stock-pile of literary language.

The emotion, moreover, often strikes us as false and even ungenerous; unless we suppose his control of language so very clumsy as to absolve him of all responsibility. The whole treatment of Hepzibah Pyncheon is an example of this. She

' began what it would be mockery to term the adornment of her person. Far from us be the indecorum of assisting, even in imagination, at a maiden lady's toilet! Our story must therefore await Miss Hepzibah at the threshold of her chamber; only presuming, meanwhile, to note some of the heavy sighs that laboured from her bosom, with little restraint as to their lugubrious depth and volume... We suspect Miss Hepzibah, moreover, of taking a step upward into a chair, in order to give heedful regard to her appearance on all sides, and full length, in the oval, dingy-framed, toilet glass, that hangs above her table. Truly! well indeed! who would have thought it! Is all this precious time to be lavished on the matutinal repair and beautifying of an elderly person...   '

This is obviously intended to be charming, as well as graceful. In between his exclamatory titterings, he describes her prayers and her kissing her brother's picture quite solemnly. But no one who reads it honestly can find it anything but offensive.

' And therefore, since we have been unfortunate enough to introduce our heroine at so inauspicious a juncture, we would entreat for a mood of due solemnity in the spectators of her fate.   '

Here again Hawthorne has miscalculated the reader's reactions with a completeness that compromises his claims to be a writer at all.

 ‘It was overpoweringly ridiculous, – we must honestly confess it – the deportment of the maiden lady while setting her shop in order for the public eye . . . Our miserable old Hepzibah! It is a heavy annoyance to a writer, who endeavours to represent nature, its various attitudes and circumstances, in a reasonably correct outline and true colouring, that so much of the mean and ludicrous should be so hopelessly mixed up with the purest pathos which life anywhere supplies to him. ’

One is tempted to accuse him of hypocrisy as well as spite, since he has gone to such lengths to make her ridiculous. But the point at issue is merely that this is bad writing, so bad as to destroy, almost by itself, all claims for Hawthorne in the genre he himself most prized.

Above all, however, it is the accents of intelligence we miss in Hawthorne's editorial voice; the companionship he offers us fails worst in its vulgarity of thought. When the stories deal with science, inventions, or magic, for instance, we find a mismating of intellectual categories which seems to imply a startling lack of understanding. Take for instance 'The Artist of the Beautiful'. Owen Warland, the Artist, is a watchmaker; but he is obsessed with the Idea of the Beautiful; so he makes a mechanical butterfly; this machine responds to thought-waves; but also to spiritual quality in a person; and its design is the result of a deep study of butterflies. This is just the kind of grotesque muddle which, in science fiction, alienates the literate reader's confidence. In the Notebooks we find 'low', 'vulgar', 'crude', 'ungentlemanly', employed as flatly and uncritically as in the worst use of the times. Key concepts like Christian and poetic are defined very genteely.

'Today I heard a dirty mother laughing and priding herself on the pretty ways of her dirty infant – just as a Christian mother might in a nursery or drawing-room.' There can be few good writers among those who equate Christianity with cleanliness, or at least among those who could write down and preserve such a sentence. Poetry he equated with unworldliness and other-worldliness. He declared that the English could not be poetic or even intellectual because they were so rosy and thick-set. 'Our pale, thin, Yankee aspect is the fitter garniture for poets.' The use of the word garniture alone hinders our listening to him with attention.

The most crucial instances of this imprecision in Hawthorne's mind, and also of that coldness of temperament which spoiled his geniality, occur when he treats the theme of the Unpardonable Sin. This sin Hawthorne most often specifies as Pride, and the critics have agreed with him, but here for once they have paid him too respectful attention. Ethan Brand is not proud. His wincing away from the vulgar crowd, his self-isolation in private thoughts, his self-dramatisation, are evidences rather of a lack of that normal pride that keeps one robustly indifferent to the world. The two characteristics common to all Hawthorne's 'proud' heroes is that they feel themselves to be cold and indifferent to other people, and that they feel they have violated the privacy of other souls by 'using' them for their own satisfaction. In other words, the emotional paralysis and the narcotic dissipation of reality which Hawthorne felt himself helplessly guilty of. The word 'Pride', like the idea of an Unpardonable Sin, and the stories of 'scientific' experiments, merely confuses the issue.

What Hawthorne in fact meant can be exemplified

from his writing a hundredfold. Here, for instance, is a passage on John Brown.

'Nobody was ever more justly hanged. He won his martyrdom fairly, and took it fairly. He himself, I am persuaded (such was his natural integrity), would have acknowledged that Virginia had a right to take the life which he had staked and lost; although it would have been better for her, in the hour that is fast coming, if she could generously have forgotten the criminality of his attempt in its enormous folly. On the other hand, any common-sensible man, looking at the matter unsentimentally, must have felt a certain intellectual satisfaction in seeing him hanged, if it were only in requital of his preposterous miscalculation of possibilities.'

There is some spite against John Brown discernible there. But the real force of that last sentence is that it is unemotional; the writer *is* in fact taking intellectual satisfaction in seeing John Brown hanged because he miscalculated the possibilities. Put this beside the contemporary official feeling for the sacredness of a man's life, which Hawthorne endorsed in a thousand places, and the remark becomes deeply shocking. This kind of sentence often escaped Hawthorne's private censorship; about the Civil War he wrote, 'I wish they would push on the war a little more briskly. The excitement had an invigorating effect on me for a time, but it begins to lose its influence.' The sentences that did not escape his censorship, those that nobody heard but himself, presumably constituted the Unpardonable Sin.

His famous remark about English women would not have been written by a Victorianly warm, or even a normal, sensibility. 'The grim, red-faced monsters! Surely a man would be justified in murdering them – in taking a sharp knife and cutting away their moun-tainous flesh until he had brought them into reasonable shape.' Or this, in a letter to his wife, 'We hold the fate of England in our hands, and it is time we crushed her – blind, ridiculous, old lump of beef, sodden in strong beer, that she is; not but what she has still vitality enough to do us a good deal of mischief, before we quite annihilate her.' Or this, about the British nation as a whole. 'They feel nothing, and bring themselves no nearer to God when they pray than when they play at cards.' This is the paralysis of the heart Hawthorne spoke of, and the violation of other people's privacy. This is what made his performance as the genial author implausible, and this is the experience he was always obliquely referring to. There was no pride in this.

But if Hawthorne was not a good writer, perhaps he was a great one. Perhaps, on his own obsessive themes, he transcended his own intentions, and delivered a profound, tragic truth. This is much more what modern critics claim for him, and it is indeed obvious that Hawthorne had some of the qualifications for writing a very remarkable book. Let us take two examples of his most celebrated tales, and try to justify our resistance to the claims made for them.

'Young Goodman Brown' is said to be a Pilgrim's Progress in reverse, an anti-Puritan allegory. But the prose is not at all evocative of such meanings; it offers no evidence that the writer knew anything about faith or morality. 'Martha Carrier, who had received the devil's promise to be queen of hell. A rampant hag was she.' Hawthorne's language refers us immediately to the world of inferior literature. Bunyan's referred us to the world of common objects, and to a system of theology and morals fervently believed in. 'On he flew among the black pines, brandishing his staff with frenzied gestures, now giving vent to an inspiration of horrid blasphemy, and now shouting forth such laughter as set all the echoes of the forest laughing like demons around him.' Nothing there evokes the experience of blasphemy. Everything evokes memories of fanciful fiction. 'Another verse of the hymn arose, a slow and mournful strain, such as the pious love, but joined to words which expressed all that our natures can conceive of sin, and darkly hinted at far more.' This is the language of empty exaggeration; after all that our natures can conceive comes 'far more'. 'Young Goodman Brown' is not an allegory because it allegorises nothing. There is no experience embodied in its language, and consequently no reason to construct elaborate meanings for its oddities. The critics' profound interpretations express their own reflections on religion and morality and doubt. Hawthorne's prose sufficiently indicates the intensity of imagination *he* put into the story.

'Ethan Brand' begins with a roar of laughter far off 'like wind shaking the boughs of a forest'. We hear the voice of children's ghost stories crudely superimposed on that of the clubman author. But it is the handling of the Unpardonable Sin, and the IDEA, which most chills our responsiveness. It seems to indicate that Hawthorne does not know the experience he is discussing first-hand, that he thinks about it as well as writing about it, all in capital letters. 'That portentous night when the IDEA was first developed' tells the reader that the author does not know what it is like to have such an idea. He seems to confuse a fascination with the moral problem of sin with philosophical inquiry in general, and that again with a practical experimentation in something like hypnotism or animal magnetism. Ethan Brand had been

'a simple and loving man, watching his fire in the years gone by, and ever musing as it burned . . . Then ensued that vast intellectual development, which, in its progress, disturbed the counter-

74

poise between his mind and heart. The Idea that possessed his
life had operated as a means of education; it had gone on culti-
vating his powers to the highest point of which they were
susceptible; it had raised him from the level of an unlettered
laborer to stand on a star-lit eminence, whither the philosophers
of the earth, laden with lore of universities, might vainly strive
to clamber after him. So much for the intellect! But where was
the heart? That, indeed, had withered, – had contracted – had
hardened – had perished! . . . he was now a cold observer, looking
on mankind as the subject of his experiment, and at length,
converting man and woman to be his puppets, and pulling the
wires that moved them to such degrees of crime as were
demanded for his study.   ’

It is not necessary to point out again the essential
identity between the character's experience and the
author's, or the incongruity of this with the story of
practical experiments, and degrees of crime, and vast
intellectual development. Quite apart from that, one
cannot respond to the passage in the way the critics
suggest because its ideas are handled ignorantly. One
cannot even assent, however passively; one must contradict. There *is* no counterpoise between the head and the
heart. Preoccupation with a moral problem does *not* give
one the kind of intellectual distinction described. The
development of the intellect does *not* mean the wither-
ing of the heart. Neither moral nor intellectual inquiry
into the nature of sin leads one into practical experiment in crime. This is all summed up in that phrase
'vast intellectual development'; as an evocation of
intellectual experience it is like 'twenty million million
diamonds' as an evocation of wealth.

The same kind of objections apply to the other
stories. 'The Birthmark' and 'Egotism; or the Bosom-
Serpent', for instance, suffer from the same emptiness
as 'Young Goodman Brown'. The moral experience
behind them is unsuccessfully integrated into their

symbolism. The Notebooks are full of entries which note, for instance, a legend about a bloody footprint, and which end, 'This could be symbolical of something'. That is the epitaph of all Hawthorne's symbolism. 'Wakefield', on the other hand, could have made a wonderful book. It was exactly Hawthorne's subject. But he didn't write it. He wrote about it instead. He turned away from the too-direct challenge. He had to disguise and muffle his guilt in the vague rhetoric of 'Ethan Brand'. 'O mankind, whose brotherhood I have cast off, and trampled thy great heart beneath my feet.'

The critics' essential claim, however, is that in a few cases, above all in *The Scarlet Letter*, Hawthorne's art, working perhaps against his own intentions, delivered a profound and tragic meaning. We cannot counter those claims point by point; partly because they are so numerous and so fully developed; but mostly because we deny their starting point. All we can do is offer some justification for that denial, for our refusal to begin to respond to the evocations of the story.

First of all, the book's claims to be historical are so insistent and so unacceptable. Hawthorne presents his seventeenth-century people as dramatically and radically unlike his readers, because of their distance in time.

'Morally, as well as materially, there was a coarser fibre in those wives and maidens of old English birth and breeding than in their fair descendants, separated from them by a series of six or seven generations; for throughout that chain of ancestry, every successive mother has transmitted to her child a fainter bloom, a more delicate and briefer beauty, and a slighter physical frame, if not a character of less force and solidity, than her own. '

This is a very crude and unhistorical version of historicity (by such a system medieval man becomes neolithic) and it has the additional disadvantage of pre-

76

scribing, or legitimising, a quite barbarous use of language for these people. Thus the children of Boston are represented as saying to each other, 'Behold, verily, there is the woman of the scarlet letter: and of a truth, moreover, there is the likeness of the scarlet letter running along by her side! Come, therefore, and let us fling mud at them.'

But when Hawthorne turns to his main characters he makes no attempt to make them 'seventeenth-century' or historically true in any sense. T. S. Eliot has said that Hawthorne's is a true criticism of the Puritan morality, true because it has the fidelity of the artist and not a mere conviction of the man, but there is very little that is Puritan in *The Scarlet Letter*. The thoughts and emotions expressed all belong to the nineteenth century. The only one of the main characters who is even said to hold Puritan beliefs is Dimmesdale, and he is a perfectly Rousseauistic hero. He is the man of sensibility. His preaching style, his physical frailty, his pallor, his eloquent, tremulous voice, his lofty brow and hollow cheek and burning eye, all these announce the romantic hero, quite incongruously translated into seventeenth-century Boston. He is no more a study in Puritanism than is Edgar Linton in *Wuthering Heights*, and the affront to our historical sense (so insistently aroused by the writer) is one of the minor sources for our distrust of the book.

More importantly, the book is full of inconsistencies. When Dimmesdale saw the scarlet letter in the sky, Hawthorne tells us that though a nation's destiny might worthily be thought to be revealed in an astronomical portent, this could not be true for an individual. He could only think he read his own fate there if he

' rendered morbidly self-contemplative by long, intense, and secret pain, had extended his egotism over the whole expanse of nature

. . . We impute it, therefore, solely to the disease in his own eye and heart, that the minister, looking upward to the zenith, beheld there the appearance of an immense letter – the letter A – marked out in lines of dull red light.   '

Quite clearly, therefore, there was no such phenomenon. But next morning the sexton says, 'But did your reverence hear of the portent that was seen last night – a great letter in the sky – the letter A?' So there was such a phenomenon, visible to others. These inconsistencies are usually explained as examples of Hawthorne's irony. That point must be answered later. For the moment let us offer only the alternative explanation that Hawthorne had not noticed his mistake.

But most important of all, since the book is said to be a study of the psychology of sin, we do not believe in Hawthorne's understanding of complex characters or emotions. Let us take Chillingworth as an example, and claim that his character does not develop during the book. We are told that he changed greatly, but we are shown nothing of it; in fact we are given evidence that he did not. A novelist who makes this kind of muddle does not have much to tell us about spiritual psychology, and we do not listen patiently to critics who attribute to him such subtle and striking intentions in, say, the scene in the forest.

We are told that when Chillingworth arrived in Boston, the day the book opens, he was calm, just, scholarly, severe, upright in all his dealings with the world, cold but kindly. Yet his first action, when Hester sees him in the crowd, was that a writhing horror twisted itself across his face, and he signed to her not to recognise him. Neither reaction is congruous with the character he is given. Such a man, cold, selfish, just, had nothing to lose by coming forward. Such a man, with no sexual passion for his wife, had no reason for a writhing horror. One can imagine, indeed, a selfish anger with Hester, for disgracing him and disappointing him of the conjugal comforts he had hoped for; one can imagine the gradual development, within that anger, of primitive passions hitherto unawakened in him; but that is not what Hawthorne describes. What is described is of the same kind of melodramatic diabolism as his behaviour at the end of the book. We are shown no development.

We are given no reason for Chillingworth's being in the Puritan settlement at all. There is no hint of religious feeling in him, in the present or the past. A scholar, remote from all emotional or practical problems, he was surely the last type of man to leave Europe for the New World. Moreover, given his view of Hester as a beautiful object and a cheering influence, it is equally difficult to understand his sending her ahead, alone, to wait two years for him in such extraordinary circumstances. Surely the most satisfactory explanation of these oddities is that Hawthorne did not think of them; because he was not dealing in human realities but in stage properties. But even if you think he was dealing in truths of the heart, and that these truths of contingency were not immediately relevant, the fact remains that an author who offers crude implausibilities of this kind forfeits our confidence.

In the scene in prison Chillingworth is shown as (implausibly) dispassionate with Hester, but implacably bent on destroying the seducer.

'"But, Hester, the man lives who has wronged us both" . . . with a smile of dark and self-relying intelligence . . . "I shall seek this man, as I have sought truth in books; as I have sought gold in alchemy . . . Sooner or later he must needs be mine!" The eyes of the wrinkled scholar glowed so intensely upon her . . . "Thine acts are like mercy," said Hester, bewildered and appalled, "but thy words interpret thee as a terror . . . Why dost thou smile at me so ?" inquired Hester, troubled at the expression of his eyes. "Art thou like the Black Man that haunts the forest round us ? Hast thou enticed me into a bond that will prove the ruin of my soul ?" "Not thy soul," he answered, with another smile, "no, not thine."   '

This is the first day of the action of the book, and Chillingworth is as diabolical as he ever becomes. He is already on the track, dark, stealthy, furious. He is already identified with the devil, with a snake, with the Black Man. He accepts that identification himself, in his last remark. Yet in chapter 10 Hawthorne says,

' He had begun an investigation, as he imagined, with the severe and equal integrity of a judge, desirous only of truth, even as if the question involved no more than the air-drawn lines and figures of a geometrical problem, instead of human passions, and wrongs inflicted on himself.   '

This is as flat a contradiction as one could find in fiction.

The next time we see Chillingworth is at the Governor's Hall, a third of the way through the book, when he is 'much uglier – how his dark complexion seemed to have grown duskier, and his figure more mis-shapen'. (This is repeated every so often throughout the book; but one hardly calls this development.) He is walking very close beside Dimmesdale, always whisper-ing in his ear, and directing significant remarks at him. 'Would it be beyond a philosopher's research, think ye, gentlemen, to analyse that child's nature, and, from its make and mould, to give a shrewd guess at the father?' By all the devices of fiction, that is, we are given to understand that he knows Dimmesdale to be Hester's seducer; or at least he suspects him and is probing his conscience. But we have not, let us note, been shown, or even told about, the birth of this suspicion. In a study of this kind, surely such a moment cries out for some kind of treatment. Hawthorne merely omits it. Nor does he, in this scene, tell us anything about the form or function of the suspicion. He parades the two men before our eyes, gives them a couple of perfunctory gestures, and whisks them away again.

His account of Chillingworth's probing, when it does come, is purely rhetorical.

‘ So Roger Chillingworth – the man of skill, the kind and friendly physician – strove to go deep into his patient's bosom, delving among his principles, prying into his recollections, and probing everything with a cautious touch, like a treasure-seeker in a dark cavern. ’

This is a picture of the idea of the thing; a reader might talk like that, describing Porfiry Petrovitch's conversations with Raskolnikov. Dostoevsky, however, did not talk like that; he gave us the reality.

Then, at this point in the book, it is insinuated – as a device of fiction it amounts to an assertion – that Chillingworth had been mixed up in the Overbury murder case, a friend of Dr Forman's, and that he had joined in evil Indian rituals. If this is true, it makes nonsense of the purity, justice, and uprightness he was credited with on arrival. If it is not true, what is it there for?

Then comes the crucial scene in which he uncovers Arthur's chest, and sees whatever he sees there, and throws his arms up and stamps on the floor and exults like the devil. We gather that he discovered something important then.

‘ After the incident last described, the intercourse between the clergyman and the physician, though externally the same, was really of another character than it had previously been. The intellect of Roger Chillingworth had now a sufficiently plain path before it. . . . Calm, gentle, passionless as he appeared, there was yet, we fear, a quiet depth of malice, hitherto latent, but active now, in this unfortunate old man.

In what sense the malice had been latent before is difficult to discover. As far as the reader is concerned (and the author is presumably addressing the reader) he has never appeared calm, gentle, or passionless; and the other characters, we have been told, instinctively felt him to be diabolical.　　　　　　　　　　　　　　　　'

'A revelation, he could almost say, had been granted to him. It mattered little, for his object, whether celestial, or from what other region. By its aid, in all the subsequent relations betwixt him and Mr Dimmesdale, not merely the external presence, but the very inmost soul, of the latter, seemed to be brought out before his eyes, so that he could see and comprehend its every movement . . . He could play upon him as he chose.　　　　'

But what had been discovered? That Arthur had been Hester's lover? He knew that before. That Arthur was suffering? He knew that. That there was a red A on Arthur's chest? This, as something extra to its meanings, which he was already sure of, could not *tell* him very much. Of course, it would be a gratification; one understands the dance of joy; but what information was conveyed, what clue given, what path was *now* opened before Chillingworth's intellect?

There is no development in the book. We are told, many times, that Chillingworth came to Boston calm and studious, and became dark and devilish. But we are not shown how this happened. We get no insight into the process. We are told that he long suspected and finally discovered that Dimmesdale was Hester's seducer; but we get no insight into the process of suspicion. We are told that he tortured his victim; but

we do not see this happen. What we do see is a fundamental confusion in Hawthorne's mind about the
characters and incidents of his fable. We have therefore
no readiness to respond to any of the book's dramatic
moments, no readiness to believe the critics when they
construct large interpretations of them.

Hawthorne himself rated *The Scarlet Letter* below *The
House of the Seven Gables*; just as he 'could not remember' what his 'blasted allegories' were about. For him
The Scarlet Letter was a 'gloomy' book, and he preferred his sunnier work. A plain reading must surely
lead us to agree with him. However, there is no hope
of convincing, with one short chapter, those who have
invested thought and emotion in an opposite valuation,
or of answering all the multifold objections that must
spring to their lips. But one point must be tackled.
Hawthorne's most complete inconsistencies are usually
dismissed by claiming that they are examples of his
irony; that he meant to keep us in doubt, for instance,
about whether there was a scarlet letter in the sky.
Hawthorne is taken to be the most ironical writer of
the nineteenth century; the only member of the New
England Renaissance too subtle to be satisfied with
Emerson's facile optimism.

It is indeed obvious that it was Hawthorne's general
policy to avoid committing himself on every issue, and
to take up more than one attitude to it. But whether,
in any particular case, this deserves the name of irony,
must depend on whether there is any point made by the
equivocation, and any evidence the writer took responsibility finally for one of the alternatives. If not, it
remains an equivocation, and, in instances like this of
the letter in the sky, a mistake. For Hawthorne certainly
was not asking us to believe that an astronomical
portent actually occurred. That would be against his

insistent practice of providing a possible natural explanation for every supernatural appearance. This time he forgot his escape route.

It is our case that there is no *a priori* reason to accept *any* ambiguity in Hawthorne as meaningful irony; that it is usually a device of caution or a carelessness. In support of that, we can point to ample evidence, in the prose, the characterisation, the narrative, that Hawthorne did occasionally make mistakes, and did habitually equivocate. We can also point to evidence of habitual naïveté.

‘ When an uninstructed multitude attempts to see with its eyes, it is exceedingly apt to be deceived. When, however, it forms its judgements, as it usually does, on the intuitions of its great and warm heart, the conclusions thus attained are often so profound and so unerring, as to possess the character of truths supernaturally revealed. ’

If a man were capable of useful irony, the sort that is a finer wisdom than Emerson's, it would prevent his saying that. When Hawthorne compares Hester on the scaffold to a Madonna and child, he continues, 'Here there was the taint of deepest sin in the most sacred quality of human woman's beauty, and the more lost for the infant that she had borne'. This is explicit and extreme. At other times, however, he takes the opposite attitude; 'what we did had a consecration of its own'. If this inconsistency is ironical, what is the point of the irony? And which was Hawthorne's final position? The questions are unanswerable. These are in fact recognisably the two halves of the stock Victorian fiction attitude to the fallen woman; public condemnation and private reverence; the incompatibility of the two in Hawthorne is due to greater naïveté, not greater sophistication.

Hawthorne's hypertrophied reputation and interpretation in modern times is no accident. It is due partly to his habit of equivocation, which made him available both for the defence of irony, and for semi-creative explanations by critics. Partly to his rejection of realism; which seemed an anticipation of the modern quest for a bolder fictional poetry, though it was in fact a retreat from the highest standards of his own day. Most of all, it is due to his quite petty and carping (because miserable) pessimism. For the last thirty years or more, all the brightest minds in American literature have been guided by an aversion from the self-consciously noble and expansive in art, the uplifting, simplifying, energising; and a corresponding enthusiasm for irony and obscurity in the method, and tragedy, pessimism, a sense of evil, in the material. We have had nearly half a century of anti-Emersonianism, and Hawthorne's reputation is one of the major forms it has taken.

Melville

and the American Romance

Richard Chase's *The American Novel and its Tradition* expounds a theory of the specifically American qualities of American fiction. This theory is not absolutely unique; it has enough in common with other theories which have inspired other contemporary critics (for instance, Marius Bewley in *The Complex Fate* and *The Eccentric Design*) for them all to be considered versions of one large idea, or at least one common sensibility. They make much the same choice of significant authors, and much the same evaluations of particular books. All the versions of this idea seem to me to take too seriously the melodramatic elements in American literature. But it will be easier to make this point if we confine ourselves to one theoretical formula, and its application to one particular author.

American fiction, Mr Chase says, is characterised by its achievement in the genre of romance, 'a freer, more daring, more brilliant fiction that contrasts with the solid moral inclusiveness and massive equability of the English novel'. If we think of the best chapters of *Moby Dick* or *The Awkward Age*, and then of the best chapters of *Middlemarch*, we grant Mr Chase's point. This is ultimately because, he continues, the American imagination has been shaped by a sense of the contradictions of Western culture, not its unities and harmonies; and this awareness of mysteries and morbidities, of extreme and eccentric states of mind, finds its natural expression in the romance, not the novel. The distinction is far from an antithesis, but it implies some different emphases in the romance. The obvious ones are sufficiently indicated just by naming the early American romance writers, Brown, Cooper, Simms, Hawthorne, Melville. But Mr Chase claims that the romance has, as well as more of the picturesque and heroic, a

'freedom from the ordinary novelistic requirements of verisimilitude, development, and continuity; a tendency towards melodrama and idyll; a more or less formal abstractness and, on the other hand, a tendency to plunge into the underside of consciousness; a willingness to abandon moral questions or to ignore the spectacle of man in society, or to consider these things only indirectly or abstractly.   '

We are reminded of Cooper's, Simms's, and Hawthorne's formulations of purpose; and of the performances of other authors, as various as Poe and Twain, all of which fit, in one way or another, into this scheme.

The romance is to be thought of as a kind of novel, but as one differing radically from the (English) norm. In his most elaborate analysis of the distinction, Mr Chase says that the romance prefers action to character, and its action will always be freer than a novel's, 'encountering, as it were, less resistance from reality'. Romance can flourish without much intricacy of relation. Its characters, probably two-dimensional types, will not be complexly related to each other, or to society, or to the past. Its human beings will on the whole be shown in *ideal* relation – 'that is, they will share emotions only after these have become abstract or symbolic'. It will not matter much what class people come from, and where the novelist would arouse our interest in a character by exploring his origin, the romancer will probably do so by shrouding it in mystery. Character itself becomes, then, somewhat abstract and ideal; so much so in some romances that it seems to be merely a function of plot; and the latter we may expect to be highly coloured.

Contrasting the American with the English tradition in another place, Mr Chase says that English fiction has been an imperial enterprise, bringing order to disorder in the new areas of experience it has described; while American fiction has rather explored, without civilising, without integrating into our everyday sensibility, its new subject matter. It has rested, aesthetically speaking, in its awareness of extreme conditions, unreconciled to any practicable morality. Among the characteristic virtues of this 'trans-Jamesian' realm of fiction are the 'intellectual energy' Brown aimed at, the Blackness of Darkness Melville found in Hawthorne, and a 'certain intrepid and penetrating dialectic of action and meaning, a radical skepticism about ultimate questions'. Among its characteristic forms have been stories of bloodthirsty adventure and scalpings, of hauntings and supernatural terrors, of ancestral curses and fearful oaths and revenges, of mad scientists and artists whose carvings come to life, of ventriloquism, somnambulism, split personality, everything spine-chilling, hair-raising, tear-wooing.

These are rich and exciting definitions. They help one to see American fiction as a whole; it becomes clear that these characteristic forms *are* found allied to serious imagination and serious literary ambition more often in American books than in British. But they also help one to see modern literature as a whole; for it is towards these characteristic virtues that all fiction has evolved in this century – one novel in which they are most splendidly achieved is *Women in Love*. Where else can one find more 'formal abstractness' combined with 'the underside of consciousness', more 'freedom from the ordinary novelistic requirements', more 'intrepid and penetrating dialectic of action and meaning, and radical skepticism about ultimate questions'?

The fact that this apotheosis of romance virtues is a work of British fiction is no set-back to Mr Chase's argument; for he insists that both kinds of fiction are to be found in both countries; it is only that a different one of the two has been dominant in each. Nor do the minor discrepancies – that one cannot easily imagine Lawrence 'shrouding a character's origin in mystery' – matter very much. They cannot be taken to prove that *Women in Love* is therefore not a romance but a novel instead. Mr Chase makes it clear that novel and romance can blend together in an infinity of ways.

However, that small discrepancy does suggest a critical point one can take more seriously. How often *does* that shrouding in mystery (typical of so much in American romance) arouse real interest in the reader – the kind of interest, that is, that forms a part of serious attention? In me it arouses mostly exasperation, even when it is done by James, Melville, or Hawthorne. And isn't there a good deal, covered by 'highly coloured plot' and 'two-dimensional types' and 'encountering less resistance from reality', a good deal we usually call Gothic, which continues to exasperate even when allied to the profoundest themes and manipulated by the most brilliant talents? Can Mr Chase really persuade us to enjoy all that staginess and sensationalism, all that nonsense – can he make it out a contributing factor of the things we do admire? And if, on the other hand, we continue to dismiss all these elements as aesthetically childish, are we not in effect rejecting his account of romance as a significant genre?

Of course a great deal remains untouched, remains convincing, in that system of definitions we began with, but haven't we removed most of that which made the term 'romance' so applicable? Does what is left deserve that name? Is there any real point in calling *Women in Love* a romance?

Mr Chase argues that critics are too ready to discuss what American literature ought to be and ought not to be, not ready enough to define what it is. His point is that American fiction *has* a romance tradition, with all kinds of consequences, good and bad. But if they should turn out to be mostly bad, is tradition the best word for them? Mr Chase sets up his American Tradition in explicit reference to F. R. Leavis's Great Tradition; if it should turn out to mean mostly a set of bad habits, should we not find some other word for it? If, more exactly, we should detect certain bad habits being handed down from one writer to another, and if those habits should be associated with Gothic material, must we not then say that romance is the wrong word for *the tradition* of American fiction? The characteristic virtues of that fiction may be what Mr Chase describes; but must they not be associated with other formal elements?

To dispute the case for all the novelists Mr Chase mentions would require a book as long as his. I have argued in other chapters that in Hawthorne and James the Gothic material does not carry the imaginative meaning successfully. If I could here make the same point about Melville, or more exactly about *Moby Dick*, I should have sufficiently substantiated my doubt. Mr Chase calls *Moby Dick* the grandest product of the American imagination, and I think most readers would agree that it is at once the most undeniable and the most peculiar of great American novels – the most defiantly unlike British fiction, and most responding, at first glance, to Mr Chase's theory. If it can be shown that *this* is not, in the important sense, a romance, my purpose will be adequately fulfilled. For I should like to repeat that it is a doubt I am substantiating. My questions are only in part rhetorical. I am not wholly convinced that Mr Chase is wrong. But neither am I convinced that he is right; and his propositions are important enough to deserve public challenge.

Mr Chase entitles one section on *Moby Dick* 'An Epic Romance'; my argument, in outline, is that much of the book can be categorised as belonging to either one or other of those two genres, and that the romance parts fail as clearly as the epic parts succeed.

That *Moby Dick* has epic elements is a commonplace of modern criticism. We need here say only that these include all the information Melville gives us about whales, and whale-men, and whale-ships; and about the craft of finding and hunting and killing whales; and about the techniques of cutting up and boiling down the blubber, and storing the oil, and so on. It includes the more general accounts of the crew; though more particularised individuals and incidents some-times serve the purposes of the romance, too (we can identify the romance, roughly, with Ahab and his maniacal quest). Thus Queequeg, Tashtego, and Daggoo have their rôles in the romance (as the savage and unwitting instruments of Ahab's lofty purpose) but on the whole they are epic figures, because they broadly and pictorially represent the diversity of nationalities and the contact with primitive cultures on all whaling ships. (Fedallah, on the other hand, with his 'one white tooth protruding from its steel-like lips', and his 'tiger-yellow' crew, is wholly a figure of romance; he is associated only with the fantastic, the sinister, the mysterious.) It is all that makes the ship and the voyage representative that is epic. Thus epic action includes most centrally the sailing and early whale hunts; but includes also the cook's sermon to the sharks, and Tashtego's near-drowning in the whale's head – incidents which have a quality of illustration and/or comic relief about them; and includes even Ishmael's meeting with Queequeg and their signing on aboard the *Pequod*, which are also treatments, in the humorous-fantastic manner, of representative aspects of the experience of whaling.

For in the epic parts Melville gives whaling an emblematic significance, as American, and democratic, and primitive. Whaling is an American preserve; whaling ships are the most democratic of ships; their crews the most international; their conditions of work the most crude. It is significant that the experience of whaling cures a hyper-civilised man of his 'hypos'; the whole story represents to its American readers a return to the source of the national virtues. The American theme was available to Melville, already embodied in epic legends, in the literature of the Frontier. The story of the White Whale itself is one of those legends; which often included heroic and semi-supernatural animals, which also featured proletarian heroes, engaged in incredible exploits, and which were diversified with grotesque humour. These legends described primitive and strenuous crafts which brought people face to face with Nature, in manly simplifications of civilised life. They were full of the sense of a people on the move and fending for itself. This sense pervades many of the chapters dealing with the *Pequod* and her crew, and helps to make them reminiscent of the Aeneid and the Odyssey.

This epic sensibility is in some ways actively hostile to the romance parts of the book, because Frontier humour was essentially levelling; it resented 'greatness' – preferred bigness, bounce, exuberance – and one of its central techniques was the reduction of the great to common dimensions. Its practitioners habitually made fun of dukes, dandies, kings, even Presidents. We should remember that Melville wrote a series of comic articles for *Yankee Doodle* in 1847 called 'Authentic Anecdotes of Old Zack' – two years before General Zachary Taylor was elected President – and so was in some degree a professional of Frontier humour. *Moby Dick* has many jokes that, for instance, draw parallels between great generals and common butchers; or between a coronation anointment of a king and the adding of an oil dressing to a salad. This kind of humour threatens Ahab's portentous dignity, his lofty superiority; not directly, but because it builds up such a broad, relaxed, open-air, Whitmanesque general attitude in the reader, quite incompatible with the feverish, theatrical shudder Ahab's curses demand.

Finally, and most important, the epic parts include nearly all the descriptions of whales and of the sea, which are the book's greatest successes. These are epic, not romance, because they are full of practical feeling; the sea is observed through a seaman's eyes – though also a poet's; the whales are watched for what they will do, how they can be killed, what they will yield. Of course this feeling is not only practical; in 'The Grand Armada' it is mostly contemplative; and in the description of the blind whale in chapter 81 pathos is dominant; but there is always also the sense of a subject known from many points of view besides that of literary sensibility. The sea is a backdrop not so much to crises of personal drama as to the life of these craftsmen and the nation they represent. As such, it can be charged with a very rhetorical excitement.

'Ship and boat diverged; the cold, damp night breeze blew

between; a screaming gull flew overhead; the two hulls wildly rolled; we gave three heavy-hearted cheers, and blindly plunged like fate into the lone Atlantic. '

But this is still a saltier sea than we find in the romance parts, for instance in the scene of the Corpusants, where it has lost its substantiality and become a largely literary effect.

This part of the book moves with the slow, wide, diffuse rhythm of epic. It has a great deal of undramatic information to convey; such drama as it has is representative; it is not about particular actions and particular individuals, but about a continuing craft and a contemporary mode of life; somewhat detached from the rest of the nation's, more primitive than the reader's own experience, but thereby more full of meaning for them. It holds a lesson for them; in the form of a picture, an emblem, of the archaic virtues. The lesson of epic is not realistic analysis, any more than it is the Byronic exaltations of romance. Thus it is quite wrong to describe the *Pequod* as a 'beautifully efficient factory for the production of whale-oil' and Ahab as 'a captain of industry', or any kind of representative nineteenth-century man. Who could be less like a captain of industry than Ahab? He is not a part of any 'picture of life'. He is a hero of romance. Even in the epic part, as soon as the *Pequod* gets deeply involved in *business* – 'all astir in the fishery', chapter 114 – Melville leaves her to it. It is the craft he is interested in, not the industry; because the craft is poetic, is epic.

Of course, all this material is not equally successful in its presentation. The information is sometimes tiresome, the moralising mechanical, the humour inept. But none of it catastrophically fails. Take, for instance, 'Stubb's Supper'; a not very successful, not very skilful, adaptation of Frontier humour; nevertheless one can read it as a part of a whole, sustained by a sense of its intention, of its natural place in a performance that as a whole succeeds.

Some features of the book do not belong to either the epic or the romance modes. Those monologues and dramatic scenes involving the mates or the crew without Ahab are fairly simply exercises in Shakespearean theatre; and Ishmael is an exception of a rather different kind. He belongs to both modes, though not without some cost to his integrity as a character, and not with equal success in each. Some American romances do have faceless narrators (Edgar Huntly and Miles Coverdale) and in some chapters of *Moby Dick* Ishmael acts as the same kind of romantic convention; for instance, his jocularity seems designed – like Coverdale's – to bridge the gap between the horrors and terrors he is narrating and the jovial narrator, drowsing over his port. But on the other hand, his style is often so boldly rhetorical and prophetic that he acts rather as the representative spectator-participant in the epic voyage of the *Pequod*. Moreover, he is out of all relation to Ahab; the two have no personal contacts, and during the chapters in which Ahab speaks, Ishmael is not present even as narrator. Those chapters are often cast in explicitly theatrical form, but even where they are not, there is no sense of Ishmael observing the events or choosing the words. This seems to me decisive. He fits into the epic parts much more fully than into the romance.

What is quite unambiguous is that Ishmael is *not* a point of view on the problems that concern Melville through Ahab. He is not (as both Richard Chase and Marius Bewley say) an alternative to Ahab in his response to Moby Dick, or to the doubloon, or to the quest. He has nothing to say on such subjects; 'The

Whiteness of the Whale' is not written in Ishmael's voice, but Melville's; he does not exist in relation to them. Indeed, after the first few chapters, Ishmael does not exist at all. His name alone survives (recurs), as a narrative device of the crudest kind. The attempt to make him into an alternative – Melville's preferred and proffered alternative – to Ahab, is a fine example of the critic's need to mythify the book he is discussing. If there *were* any unity between the epic and the romance parts of *Moby Dick*, it would no doubt *be* by means of Ishmael. But in point of fact there is no such unity; magnificent as some parts are, the book does not exist as a whole; the two genres function on different levels of the imagination, and also in different directions. Ishmael's disintegration and disappearance is one of the marks of this.

In the romance parts, Ahab is of course the main character, and the most purely romantic. There are some attempts to explain him in terms of parentage, religion, and calling, but the dominant stress is on his inexplicability. The characteristic note in his presentation is the superhuman. Moreover, though Melville invokes some Shakespearean parallels – equipping him with Pip, for instance – it is Ethan Brand we associate Ahab with rather than King Lear. He is essentially of humble birth. It is his thoughts alone that are haughty. His grandeur is enveloped in lurid mystery, and free from the taint of wealth or privilege. Thus he is a typical figure of American romance. And around him are grouped his more simply lurid subordinates, Fedallah, Pip, and Elijah, the prophet of Nantucket (Gabriel of the Jeroboam is an epic treatment of essentially the same material).

Romance action includes Ahab's monologues, his address to the whale's head, the swearing of the oath, the drinking from the harpoon sockets, the tempering of the blade in blood, the smashing of the quadrant. It includes also those mysteries, like the figures flitting along the Nantucket quay the morning the *Pequod* sailed, and Ahab's non-appearance till late in the voyage, which are subsequently explained as due to natural causes. Those explanations themselves are of the essence of romance as written by Hawthorne and Brown.

Some of these scenes are cast in theatrical form, and look very like that Shakespearean material which is not really either epic or romance. The Shakespearean exercises, however, are nearly always comic; Ahab's tragic monologues are really scenes of romance with Elizabethan trimmings. Romance was a genre that used many trimmings – eclectic devices to heighten effect – and was always especially drawn to drama. Dostoevsky, for instance, the greatest of all transformers of Gothic material into serious art, concentrated his scenes within unities of time and space that overtly remind us of the theatre. *The Idiot*, in particular, is in effect a play in novel form, as George Steiner reminds us in *Tolstoy or Dostoevsky?* This is because the movement of romance is essentially rapid, concentrated, a sequence of tensions and explosions; the stories concern individuals, and are full of personal conflicts, or enormous personal decisions; the reality of the outside world and social groups is drastically diminished. Larger units of time and place (dominant in epic) scarcely exist.

The discontinuity between the two modes, epic and romance, is somewhat masked by the continuity of Melville's rhetoric. He had worked out (drawing on Carlyle and others) a high prophetic style, genialferocious in tone, rich in metaphor and metonymy and all the flowers of rhetoric, which could be applied to both modes with no major modifications.

But that there is a disjunction is very clear in those

passages where Melville explains why Ahab, despite his 'grand monomania', did in fact go whaling in the normal manner, even after the Quarter-Deck scene; or why, despite the crew's crude and earthy natures, they could get caught up in this crazy idealistic quest. It is not so much that there are such passages, but that they are so uneasy in tone. Melville is conscious of a profound difficulty. Chapter 46, 'Surmises', offers us six possible reasons why Ahab went on hunting other whales after the crew had sworn to pursue Moby Dick alone. The true reason is of course that Melville is writing two books, one of which is about whaling.

'The Affidavit' attempts rather similarly to 'take away any incredulity which a profound ignorance of the entire subject may induce in some minds, as to the natural verity of the main points of this affair'. But it is not that there *could* be a whaling captain like Ahab that troubles the reader, but that there *was*; not that a ship might set out in pursuit of such a whale, but that this one did; not that a whale might sink a ship, but that the voyage of the *Pequod* ever took place. We doubt that any of the romance part of the book ever happened – we feel, that is, that Melville never imagined it, as opposed to fancied it – played with the idea. Our reason is that so much of it fails to impose itself on *our* imaginations.

It fails first of all because the language becomes so grotesquely distended. ' "The black vomit wrench thee!" ' and ' "Curses throttle thee!" yelled Ahab', and ' "Avast!" roared Ahab, dashing him against the bulwarks.' No serious meaning could be conveyed in such language; it is good for nothing but pulp magazines; it serves that absolutely undiscriminating taste for melodrama which we symbolise by the term 'pulp-magazine'. ' "Death and devils! Men, it is Moby Dick ye have seen – Moby Dick – Moby Dick!" ' . . . Tossing both arms, with measureless imprecations he shouted out.' Surely that last sentence describes just what Melville is doing in such passages. And though this language is not often *merely* foolish – it is one of literature's great feats of rhetoric – it is always *foolish*; for at its best it celebrates the writer's intention and not his subject.

' . . . and thus chase away, for that one interval, the clouds that layer upon layer were piled upon his brow, as ever all clouds choose the loftiest peaks to pile themselves upon . . . The thick plaits of his forehead relaxed . . . His firm lips met like the lips of a vice; the Delta of his forehead's veins swelled like over-laden brooks; in his very sleep, his ringing cry rang through the vaulted hull, "Stern all, the White Whale spouts thick blood". '

This is superb in a way, but its effect of size is categorically larger than life; and in all those superb images of Ahab as a natural phenomenon, in all his grandest rhetoric, in all those successions of rich monosyllables, we never begin to think of Ahab as a fully real, fully imagined person, in some sense independent of the language used about him. The obvious contrast is Moby Dick; Melville magnifies the White Whale, too, but without losing contact with simple realism; Moby Dick is made meaningful to us in many different modes, but they are all consonant with each other and with the simplest factuality. Ahab is a figure purely of melodrama, and casts an unreal theatrical light on whatever he comes in contact with.

' But what it was that inscrutable Ahab said to that tiger-yellow crew of his -- these were words best omitted here; for you live under the blessed light of the evangelical land. Only the infidel sharks in the audacious seas may give ear to such words, when, with tornado brow, and eyes of red murder, and foam-glued lips, Ahab leaped after his prey. '

Here (in constructions significantly reminiscent of 'Young Goodman Brown') we even begin to lose faith in the sea and its fish themselves, so self-intoxicated is the rhetoric, so self-limited to cheap theatre. And yet the sea, the whale-boat, the whale-hunt, have been made incomparably real to us before, in the epic chapters; Ahab himself, who exists only in the romance parts, never begins to come to life.

This is not simply a matter of the choice of words and images. It is a matter also of the information given us about him, the gestures assigned to him, the scenes in which he appears; so much of which is inappropriate to anything more serious than a pulp-magazine hero.

'Threading its way out from among his grey hairs, and continuing right down one side of his tawny scorched face and neck, till it disappeared in his clothing, you saw a slender rod-like mark, lividly white . . .   '

and then the contradictory, but equally lurid, accounts of the origin of this mark; it is simply bad reading to respond to this with anything more serious than the conventional shiver of excitement. And though the critics tell us that this shiver is the beginning of a profound response, that this theatricality is merely the most obvious aspect of a richly imagined whole, what we in fact find in the total treatment of Ahab is clumsiness, uncertainty, and self-dramatisation. It is surely very clumsy to have him 'muttering to himself' such long literary sentences as he 'turns into his cabin'; or to have him advancing upon Stubb with 'such overbearing terrors in his aspect' in order to say, 'Then be called ten times a donkey, and a mule, and an ass, and begone, or I'll clear the world of thee'. In all such scenes Melville most clumsily reminds us of the inherent limitations of the Gothic style. It is surely uncertainty which produces so many excuses for Ahab's behaving like a normal captain occasionally. 'Though of all men the moody captain of the *Pequod* was the least given to that sort of shallowest assumption . . .', two more clauses beginning 'though . . .' and then, 'yet even Captain Ahab was by no means unobservant of the paramount forms and usages of the sea. . . .' Men, Melville adds apologetically, have to use 'some sort of external arts or entrenchments, always, in themselves, more or less paltry and base'. It is uncertainty we hear in 'Unwittingly here a secret has been divulged, which perhaps might more properly, in set way, have been disclosed before'. This is the true explanation of Ahab's non-appearance at Nantucket. 'But, in the end, it all came out; this one matter did, at least. That direful mishap was at the bottom of his temporary exclusiveness.' And it is self-dramatisation we hear in 'Oh, Starbuck! Is it not hard that with this weary load I bear, one poor leg should have been snatched from under me? Here, brush this old hair aside; it blinds me, that I seem to weep. Locks so grey did never grow but from out some ashes. But do I look so very old, so very very old, Starbuck? I feel . . .' This is someone pretending to be an actor, a Shakespearean hero, in front of his mirror. 'Waving his hand, he moves away from the window.'

It is this fickle, fitful, semi-personal involvement of an author in his character we feel in Ahab; not the sustained, steady, self-forgetful effort of creativity. There is no total reality there, of which the Gothic melodrama could be the crudest aspect, or from which it could be a lapse. He is of course given some lines that transcend all ordinary fiction – 'I see in him outrageous strength, with an inscrutable malice sinewing it' – but his other lines, his gestures, his life-story, his behaviour on the voyage, do not build this up. They are imaginatively incongruent with it. They do not build anything up, except a Gothic fiction which does not offer itself as real in any sense, but as something about which or through which the author can express his serious meaning. This was, after all, Melville's creative pattern. He was, as Newton Arvin says, the least inventive of writers, the most convertive or transmutative; he habitually took some true narrative or encyclopaedia entry, and embellished and moralised about it – 'wrote it up', in that grand Carlylean rhetoric that really was, at its best, a major creative mode. Where he is simply inventing, as in *Mardi* or in the London episode of *Redburn*, the strain is palpable. And in *Moby Dick* he worked as usual; in the romance parts as well as in the epic; only the given entity around which he was writing was in the former not fact but fiction. Melville always disclaims responsibility for this 'given entity'; the creative work, he implies, is what he says about that, the truths of the imagination he can show us symbolically rendered there. But while his fact (sea-voyaging) is interesting in itself, and most of it imaginatively known to the author, his fiction (Gothic romance) is of a cheap kind, and arouses the author's impulses to windiness and self-intoxication. The sea, therefore, exists in the book as a whole, independent of the particular moral Melville may be drawing from it in a particular place; so do the whales; so does Moby Dick; but Ahab and the *Pequod*'s quest do not. Melville admits as much over and over again. When Ahab yields to Starbuck after first overruling him, Melville says, 'It were, perhaps, vain to surmise exactly why it was, that as respecting Starbuck, Ahab thus acted. It may have been . . .' The tortured syntax again betrays the truth. Melville does not *know* why Ahab does the things he does. Because he has not fully imagined him. He has not fully imagined any of the mates. He keeps losing the distinction between Stubb and Flask. He tells us after 200 pages that 'Stubb was one of those odd sort of humourists whose jollity is sometimes so curiously ambiguous, as to put all inferiors on their guard in the matter of obeying them'; but this insight is not incorporated into the figure of Stubb; it is not seen or heard in him before or after. Why does Bulkington disappear from the ship? Why does Ishmael cease to be the narrator? Why does Queequeg cease to be an individualised character? Why does the *Pequod* have sometimes a wheel and sometimes a tiller? Why is Stubb sometimes the second and sometimes the third mate? The answer to all these questions is that Melville changed his mind about dozens of features of the *Pequod*'s voyage, and did not think it important to go back and revise. It is not important because the voyage never really happened; it never became a real event in his mind; it remained an occasion for creative writing.

This vitiates much of the serious discussion of the book. For instance, Marius Bewley says that 'the whole complex movement' starts from Ahab's loss of his leg; but one is bound to protest that neither the event nor the man is real enough, or consistent enough, to give meaning to that assertion. Melville's account of Ahab and his motives varies from chapter to chapter. Elijah's prophecies, for instance, hint at other things in Ahab's early life – such as the deadly scrimmage with the Spaniard before the altar at Santa. But more important, can one imagine Ahab with two legs? He is rendered, so much of the time, purely as an attitude towards having only one; he doesn't exist as a person with other possibilities. He is not a real character, and one cannot extrapolate events or motives for him outside the book. He is a fiction, something conjured up to serve the writer's multifarious purposes – purposes which may have changed quite importantly by the next chapter, so that we get a quite different explanation of him.

This is, moreover – to return to our argument with Mr Chase – exactly the weakness of American romance as a genre. As practised by Hawthorne, for example, romance tells its readers not that something exciting happened, but that it may have happened. A scarlet letter may have appeared in the sky over Boston. The romancer feels free to imply fairly seriously both that it did and that it didn't. This is one of the freedoms of romance – one of its differences from the novel. And collaterally, romance can invent persons and incidents of the most lurid kind ('highly coloured') and enjoy the immediate excitement they generate, without feeling committed (another freedom) to develop or give meaning to that excitement, provided it can afterwards, however mechanically, explain them away. Thus the reader has the thrill of supernatural events – the shadowy figures flitting along the quay – without being asked to believe in them.

This is a weakness of specifically American romance. For the romance tradition, so far from being strong in America, was in fact feebler there than in other literatures. Emily Brontë, for instance, avoided this debilitating equivocation, this disastrous split between fact and fancy. Everything in *Wuthering Heights*, however melodramatic, even supernatural, quite simply and firmly happens. Dostoevsky, by his love of newspaper fact, his skill in newspaper naturalism, managed to transcend the limitations – the sensibilitarianism – of even *Wuthering Heights* romance. One need only compare Starbuck and his gun beside the sleeping Ahab – so feebly Shakespearean – with, for instance, Raskolnikov and his axe outside the moneylender's door, to realise how poor a variety of romance American Gothic was.

But above all (from the point of view of the present argument), *Moby Dick* fails in certain essential, ineluctable, structural ways, as a result of Melville's fiction being romance-as-such. The successful parts described were after all background; a foreground was needed, as in the Aeneid or the Odyssey – a particular voyage, a particular captain, some large catastrophe or triumph, treated as foreground. Epic too needs its hero, as much as romance or the novel. The legend of the White Whale is the right kind of connecting link, and Moby Dick himself is one of the great things in world literature – the great protagonist of Nature, or Life, in all its awesome, archaic, unmasterable power. But even if Melville had been a more skilful writer; even if American romance had been a better variety of the genre; still Ahab and the *Pequod*'s quest would have failed as epic foreground, just because Melville refused to 'treat' manners, character, or human relationships; because of the romance-writer's 'willingness to abandon moral questions or to ignore the spectacle of man in society'. Mr Chase himself remarks that the Odyssey is far more novelistic than *Moby Dick*; because of its far more sophisticated interest in manners and behaviour. The crudity of Melville's uninterest is ruinous to epic as much as to ordinary fiction. In the chapter 'The Cabin-Table', for instance, he has a chance to show us Ahab's social personality; his relations to Starbuck and Stubb; their relations to each other. He has a chance to give all these characters a new dimension of reality – one they badly need after the sustained implausibility of scenes like 'The Quarter-Deck'. But, following the prescriptions of romance, this chapter again shows us Ahab as 'a mute maned sea-lion on the white coral beach, surrounded by his warlike but still deferential cubs'; and, at the other extreme, Flask as a sort of Shakespearean clown. The romance hero is always

106

heroic, and usually touched with the supernatural –
never engaged in life-sized activity. All social life
appears in Melville as 'some sort of external arts and
entrenchments, always, in themselves, more or less
paltry and base'. A fair cartoon of this is the scene of
magnetising the new compass, where Ahab for once
does act out of less then heroic motives.

‘ Then going through some small strange motions with it –
whether indispensable to the magnetizing of the steel, or merely
intended to augment the awe of the crew, is uncertain, Ahab
. . . etc. (The crew slink away, duly awed.) . . . In his fiery eyes
of scorn and triumph, you then saw Ahab in all his fatal pride. ’

This is about as close as Melville can come to the play
of mixed and humble motives in human relationship;
and surely it is this gap which makes the book so
radically incomplete. The gap which is made manifest
in the mates (think what George Eliot would have
made of Starbuck), and wherever the intensities of
pride, despair, insight (even if better rendered) need to
be related to everyday concerns; and wherever the
tragic manner (even if more successful) has to handle
humble facts. This is the book's essential failure, and
it is directly due to Melville's whole approach to fiction
– to his being a writer of romances-and-not-novels.

For all these reasons, surely Mr Chase is wrong to
imply that the 'tradition' of romance in American
fiction was a source of Melville's strength.

There were traditions in American literature that did
help him, of course. The material stored up in Frontier
legend and Frontier humour was one. Another was that
Carlylean-Emersonian moralising rhetoric, with its
taste for Sir Thomas Browne and seventeenth-century
baroque prose, and its links with the sermon – Father
Mapple's address is surely Melville's most successful

short form. But if one considers Melville's career as a whole, what one is more struck by is the *lack* of useful traditions, his floundering and repeated failures to translate imaginative insights into aesthetic wholes; despite an intellectual energy and a command of language in many ways really superb. He worked within a tradition, true; but that tradition betrays him, before our eyes, over and over again. The creative habits Melville inherited from Hawthorne, in that most pathetic of all affiliations, were nearly all bad.

I should like to illustrate this from the short story, 'Cock-a-doodle-doo!'; not that it is more vivid there than elsewhere (a more vividly floundering failure than *Pierre* would be too painful to describe) and not that it is the very best of his stories, but just that it is neglected and misunderstood. It was published the same year as 'Bartleby' and is not incomparable with it in quality, but the critics seem to have all wilfully misunderstood it.

It is surely wilful to interpret a story as being about Emersonian self-reliance, when the principal character is called Merrymusk, and his principal feature is that he 'possesses an extraordinary cock'. The crowing fo this cock is described in richly sexual language, as

‘ so vast, mounting, swelling, soaring, as if spurted out from a golden throat, thrown far back . . . a jolly bolt of thunder with bells to it . . . clear, shrill, full of pluck, full of fire, full of fun, full of glee . . .   ’

When the narrator hears this cock-crow, he is overjoyed and sees life in wholly new colours; but this is no gently lyrical inspiration; it is a call to hard self-assertion and disregard of the rest of the world.

‘ But next morning, again I heard the inspiring blast, again felt my blood bound in me, again felt superior to all the ills of life, again felt like turning my dun out of doors.

Plain as a cock could speak, it said, "Let the world and all aboard of it go to pot. Do you be jolly, and never say die. What's the world compared to you? What is it anyhow, but a lump of loam? Do you be jolly." ,

The narrator goes off in search of this cock, thinking first it must be the property of the rich and respectable, but in vain. He then asks Merrymusk, a man who cuts wood for him, if he knows any gentleman nearby who owns an extraordinary cock.

6 The twinkle glittered plain in the wood-sawyer's eye.
"I know of no *gentleman*," he replied, "who has what might well be called an extraordinary cock." ,

This Merrymusk is a remarkable foreshadowing of Oliver Mellors.

6 He was tall and spare, with a long saddish face, yet somehow a latently joyous eye, which offered the strangest contrast . . . He never spoke unless spoken to. He only sawed . . . He was mum. He came to saw my wood, and eat my dinners – if I chose to offer them – but not to gabble . . . I increased the respectfulness and deferentialness of my address towards him. I concluded within myself that this man had experienced hard times; that he had had many sore rubs in the world. ,

He has been a sailor, like Melville, and ran away from his ship in the East Indies; he is now married, but his wife is sick, and his children are ailing; they are extremely poor, but content, and even joyful, because of Merrymusk's extraordinary cock. The narrator finally tracks down the crowing, and discovers the cock.

6 "Good heavens! do you own the cock? Is that cock yours?"
"Is it my cock!" said Merrymusk, looking slyly gleeful out of the corner of his long solemn face. ,

He refuses to sell it, which makes him in the eyes of the narrator a rich man despite his material poverty.

'I stood awhile admiring the cock, and wondering at the man. At last I felt a redoubled admiration of the one, and a redoubled deference for the other . . . "You seem a glorious independent fellow", said I.'

The cock's name is Trumpet, and though its crowing seems so unsuitable in a sick-room ('I leaped from my chair. The cock frightened me, like some overpowering angel in the Apocalypse') the wife and the children continually beg to see him and hear him crow. They 'sun themselves in the radiant plumage', and the cock 'glorifies and irradiates' the shack. Their faces shine out through the grime and pallor 'as if they were the children of emperors'. The narrator is doubtful about this reckless self-assertion and social irresponsibility, and the whole family in fact dies of sickness and poverty; but the cock lives on undiminished in its vitality, its splendour, and then expires in mid-crow. The narrator buries them all beneath a grave-stone with not a skull and crossbones, but 'a lusty cock in the act of crowing, chiseled on it'. And he is never down-hearted again.

You can find, in critical journals, elaborate cases made out for this story being a satire on Thoreau's *A Week on the Concord and Merrimack Rivers*; or a satire on 'Resolution and Independence'; not only ignoring the cock's sexual meaning, but arguing that the writer is criticising its naïve self-confidence. But if literary scholarship means anything at all, there is surely no need to argue such interpretations point by point. What Melville means by the cock is after all closely related to what he expressed in the whale; both are misread for the same reason – that people have been taught to expect only black truths from Melville. It is more surprising that Newton Arvin should describe the cock as a 'perfunctory' symbol of courage and cheerfulness triumphing over defeat and death. The word is used in the sexual sense in Shakespeare and the Rabelais translations Melville was so fond of; Merrymusk is just his kind of pun; and there is plenty of evidence of his fondness for elaborate and hidden sexual jokes.

But when Mr Arvin goes on to describe this story (and others) as 'painfully concocted and convictionless', we are bound to agree. The narrator essays that jaunty club-man tone, and the narrative line wanders in that feeble and uncontrolled way, which we know so well in Melville. Which we know in Hawthorne, too; for they belong to American romance as a genre. The feebly jaunty, would-be rakish first person (let's puff a cigar together, sir, and to the devil with our duns) was one of the ways romancers bridged the gap between the marvels they recounted, and the public they addressed. (Emily Brontë's Mr Lockwood and Conrad's Marlowe are related ways of doing the same thing.) The wandering narrative line, which elaborates tiny events and slides through big ones, which mingles together things of every shade of plausibility, is the natural profile of an incompletely imagined fiction. The writer does not maintain his criteria of reality from one page to the next; he does not ask himself what the event or tone of one paragraph will look like from the point of view of the next.

The basic insight of 'Cock-a-doodle-doo!' is bold and beautiful; and if it is less centrally Melvillean than that of 'Bartleby', this story as a whole perhaps suffers less than the other one from the feebleness and absurdity of half its elements. It suffers less, but it is hideously maimed. Taken together, anyway, the two stories offer a satiric comment on the usual pieties of

Melville scholarship; 'The first works to be touched with the influence of Hawthorne's stories were *Moby Dick* and *Pierre*, but hard upon the almost universal condemnation of *Pierre* in 1852, Melville was offered work in Hawthorne's own delicate medium'. He began, that is, to write stories like 'Cock-a-doodle-doo!' and 'Bartleby', in which most vivid inspirations were ruined by the form into which they were translated.

Hawthorne's fructifying influence on *Moby Dick* can be identified more or less with the Gothic elements we have discussed; and his responsibility for *Pierre* alone would make our case. But let us look back to *Redburn* a moment, and to the figure of Jackson there; where Melville came so close to fully rendering – in *fictional* terms – the kind of human evil that obsessed him; in the last piece of fiction he worked on before that influence. Wasn't he nearer there, using the techniques of the novel, than he ever got in romance to presenting the black possibilities of human relationship? Can one think his discipleship to Hawthorne anything but an enormous misfortune? Can one believe that the tradition of romance helped make *Moby Dick*, or any other American fiction, great?

Twain and Whitman

the problem of 'American' literature

‘ I put my hand on the sun's face and make night on the earth;
I bite a piece out of the moon and hurry the seasons: I shake
myself and crumble the mountains. ’

If that were set out as verse, no one would hesitate to
accept it as Whitman's, but in point of fact it comes
from the boatman's boast in *Old Times on the Mississippi*.
With minor variations, it could have come from *Moby
Dick*, *Walden*, a Davy Crockett almanac, or an issue
of *The Spirit of the Times*; for this is the generically
American style, evolved in the early nineteenth century
in the most non-literary contexts, inherited and trans-
formed later by the serious imaginative writers. Twain
and Whitman are far from the most alike of the
inheritors, but they deserve to be considered together
because they best exemplify, first the handicaps this
rich endowment brought with it, and second the difficulties it presents to the modern reader, even trans-
formed. To judge by contemporary criticism, our
responses to 'American' literature – if we can use that
term to describe all the serious books importantly
deriving from that heritage – have more of confusion
and unreason in them than any others.

The origin of this style, and the whole tradition of

literary forms and cultural meanings it expressed, have received much scholarly attention lately; this is very valuable, for they are probably the crucial facts of American literary history; and it perhaps permits us to refer to them in brief.

Summarily, then, this style was humorous in tone, but included strong and savage feelings; it was characterised by a very assertive, exuberant, rhapsodic, use of 'I', as a mouthpiece not for one person, but for a whole crowd, an audience; it alternated the grandest language (and thoughts) with the most homely – specialising in both crude dialect and poetic rhetoric; it swung fast between hyperbole and burlesque, often in a third realm, where the two were not mutually exclusive; it achieved verbal conceits bolder than anything in the contemporary orthodox literature. The literary forms included the stage monologue, the comic lecture, the stock character (the Yankee Peddler, the Negro, the Backwoodsman, the Confidence Man), and the tall tale, sometimes involving the legendary or even the supernatural. The characteristic meanings included a profound melancholy, a savage satire, a devastating cynicism, an irrepressible vitality, a preoccupation with death and cruelty and horror, above all an exultant participation in the 'people', the uncultured, unprivileged, irresponsible commonalty, triumphantly asserting its own autonomy far from the centres of propriety and privilege.

A large literature (or anti-literature) of this kind arose in America in the 1820s, '30s, and '40s, and produced its effect immediately on the serious writing of the time. This was not surprising, given the enthusiasm of contemporary literary theory for the primitive, the wild, the legendary, the epic. Indeed the non-literary originators of the style, and even the people they wrote *about*, were conscious of their ideological glamour;

backwoodsmen would refer to themselves as 'Children of Nature', invoking Rousseau. The serious writers were alive to the opposite, genteel tradition (I would use that term to include novels like Cooper's *Satanstoe*) but the crucial fact of American literary history is that the Frontier tradition produced the more exciting writing of the two. Each was profoundly conscious of the other; each could be described as a series of gestures aimed at the other; but the Frontier writers had captured the masculine and glamorous rôle. (Mark Twain's marriage is in many ways an apt metaphor for the relationship between the two traditions.) This was to be expected from the general intellectual trends of the times, but it also dramatically 'happened' in specific areas of literature.

The most striking example occurs in the line of South-Western humorists, from Augustus Baldwin Longstreet to George Washington Harris. (Kenneth S. Lynn treats this in detail in *Mark Twain and South-western Humor*.) These men all wrote anecdotes about the lazy, ignorant, dangerous, Democrat, proletarians of their region, from the point of view of educated, gentlemanly Whig narrators. But as we pass from book to book, both within the line, and within a particular writer's work, it becomes obvious how all the vitality and interest and even pathos was gradually absorbed by the figures who were originally set up to be mocked at and warned against. This kind of writing and this shift of values spread across the country. Twain's 'The Dandy and the Squatter', written when he was 17, is a typical anecdote of the humiliation of a superior, elegant, cityman by a rough South-Westerner, but it was reprinted in a Boston paper, where it would be read by far fewer squatters than dandies.

Melville is no doubt the most obvious, as well as the most brilliant, user of this style, these legends, these stock characters, these moods. But Poe found there some of his cruel comedy, his fascination with death, his fantastic inventions, his newspaper hoaxes. And the language Emerson evolved for Transcendentalism, and Thoreau developed, had the same alternation of the most noble and abstract thoughts with the most concrete and practical, the same assertive expansiveness of tone, the same impudence that deliberately affronts discursive decorum and reverses the reader's expectations, the same aspiration to the epic.

Twain and Whitman can however claim to represent this inheritance more fully than anybody else, because they derived from it their sense of their rôle as writer. All the others derived much more of that sense from the orthodox literature of the past, and therefore handled the Frontier heritage somewhat from the outside. (I would distinguish here between Whitman's sense of his rôle, and his idea of it; the latter, obviously, was of the grandest: but what in fact guided his choice of particular gesture was something different.) This is partly to be explained by the fact that they were newspapermen. Though this cultural tradition dramatised itself as belonging to the Frontier, it was in fact as much allied to the Press. Most of the South-Western humorists wrote for newspapers, and this material all made its first appearance in magazines and was reprinted from one into another across the country. It was newspapermen who ghost-wrote Davy Crockett's books for him, and who created half the legends of the West. The Frontier was in fact allied to several branches of entertainment and publicity. It was on the popular stage (so unsympathetic to people like Emerson and Thoreau, but where Twain and Whitman were so much at home) that most of the stock characters, in all their broad coarse humour, were first invented.

Even more important is that the original tradition was *not* allied to orthodox literature – was in many ways anti-literary, burlesquing conventional forms, dramatising its own uncouthness, hostile to the pronouncements of critics and professors – hostile to everything Henry James and Matthew Arnold came to stand for. Twain and Whitman were of course sworn enemies of the latter, and very uncertain of their own relation to literature proper. They were half the time ready to question the existence of any critical standard, the other half ready to submit to its harshest interpretation and declare their own work worthless. They had a much weaker sense than the other writers of belonging to a literary world. It is, for instance, Poe's preoccupation with pure literary values that marks the limit of his participation in the Frontier heritage, despite his newspaper work.

But above all, writers like Melville and Hawthorne, Emerson and Thoreau, could use only fragments of this material, and must then transform it, because they were not temperamentally at home in crowds, in the world of the political convention, or the law courts, or the newspaper office. These were the contexts of origin of this material; it was at local bar association meetings in the South-West that half the comic anecdotes first gained currency; and they needed a crowd-audience to have their full effect. These writers could not identify themselves with a real crowd, or write so as to make it identify itself with them. *Their* protests against the genteel tradition, their love of the heroic and the primitive, their use of the American style, had to be in the service of a deeply solitary personality.

In consequence, it is in Twain and Whitman that we find the purest examples of the literary difficulties this material brought with it – along with such brilliance of language, such freshness of feeling, such political and mythical rightness. And it is in our treatment of them that we feel most clearly our own paralysis before a certain kind of literary problem.

First let us remind ourselves how much is implied in saying that Twain and Whitman were newspapermen; and that the cultural tradition behind the American style owed much to the worlds of journalism, entertainment, and publicity.

Both Twain and Whitman were apprenticed to printing in a newspaper office as soon as they left school, and were writing pieces for their own papers from the age of twelve or so; their pieces were early reprinted, Twain's in a Boston paper when he was 17, Whitman's in a New York paper when he was 15. They in effect grew up in newspaper offices and got their education there. Whitman was an editor himself at 23, and both retained all their lives a familiarity with, even fondness for, the processes of publicity, which distinguishes them sharply from most literary men (compare Henry James's attitude to publicity, in *The Bostonians*, for instance) and aligns them with figures of Frontier legend. All the heroes of the Frontier were involved in a process of legend-making, in which truth and fiction were inextricably mixed; the archetypal case is that of Kit Carson finding among the wreckage of a waggon pillaged by Indians a dime-novel relating the exploits of the Indian scout, Kit Carson; and the publicity became an essential part of their personalities.

Twain and Whitman commanded also a flow of that editorial rhetoric that makes a reader feel that he is just one of the crowd, but just as good as anyone else all the same. This again is something instinctively distasteful to most literary men, but the stock in trade of the heroes of the West, and in quite an extreme form. For this was no genteel literary journalism. In 1835,

118

the year of Twain's birth and of Whitman's first arrival in New York, James Gordon Bennett founded the *New York Herald* as the first independent paper costing a penny, and inaugurated the era of the most uninhibited newspaper enterprise. The stridency of tone and vulgarity of manner, the demagoguery and social aggressiveness, were where the word journalism got its worst associations. The effect of this world, as a training ground, as an education, on men with the sensibilities of imaginative writers, was necessarily profound.

The political sensibility, for instance, of both Twain and Whitman bore the imprint of that training. Sentimentally fervent democrats, they could be completely cynical about both human nature and political institutions. They were very much at home in the intrigues of party leaderships and political conventions, but cherished the most innocent hopes for a non-politician to lead the country, a man of the people, all soldierly simplicity and vernacular nobility. They were devoted to General Grant, the Eisenhower of his time, and in the teeth of the scandals of his administrations.

Then their kind of exultance in their country, their era, and the future, was nearer to the tone of an editorial than that of other serious writers. It was to Whitman Twain wrote on his birthday in 1889 that he had lived 'just the seventy years which are greatest in the world's history'. Their attitude to the past, to Europe, to all traditional values, was often both philistine and vulgar.

‘ Of the twenty four modern mammoth two-double, three-double, and four-double cylinder presses in the world, printing by steam, twenty one of them are in the United States. ’

This is from Whitman's Letter to Emerson in 1856. What other serious writer could have written it? Hardly the addressee: perhaps only Twain.

' We shall presently be indifferent to being looked down upon by a nation no bigger and no better than our own [England]. We made the telegraph a practical thing; we invented the fast press, the sewing machine, the sleeping and parlor car, the telephone, the ironclad, we have done our share for the century, we have introduced foretelling of the weather. '

This comes from Twain's Notebook. There is plenty of 'Americanism' in Melville, Emerson, Hawthorne, but to find it basing itself on such unequivocal material-ism, you would have to go outside the ranks of the imaginative writers, to someone like Andrew Carnegie – a friend of Twain's and patron of Whitman's, inci-dentally. Or to some popular orator in the Frontier tradition.

They belonged to that tradition in the good ways, too, however. Both had, for instance, a marked affinity with Lincoln. Whitman's feeling for the dead President, and his self-identification with the national cult, is a part of his literary product. But that feeling was more than sentimental and literary. His description of an ideal President in 'The 18th Presidency!' in 1856, exactly fits the figure Lincoln made of himself in 1860 and after. There was a genuine unity between them. While Twain ('the Lincoln of our literature', as Howells called him) inherited the lighter side of Lincoln's rôle as backwoods sage in polite society, Twain and Lincoln are America's two supreme public figures in the Frontier tradition of humour.* Lincoln found there his fund of fables and dirty jokes, his skill in telling stories, his pose of naïveté, his conscious drawl, his melancholy, his sudden savagery, his power of burlesque – he once mimicked a political opponent so closely and savagely, in front of him and a crowd,

* There are more links than an Englishman expects between that tradition and political life in America; Twain was himself a kind of political oracle in his later years, as was Davy Crockett before him, and Will Rogers after.

in every phrase and tone and gesture, that the man was reduced to public tears. The affinity worked in the other direction, too. Lincoln read *Leaves of Grass* – one of the few who did – and was impressed – one of a still smaller number. He died before Twain's work was known, but he was a great admirer of Artemus Ward and Petroleum V. Nasby. These three, Lincoln, Whitman, Twain, as statesman, prophet, entertainer, stand together and express the same America, in a way hardly anyone else can equal. Emerson, Melville, Hawthorne, all spoke for and to a much more limited audience. Twain's and Whitman's admirers (Bernard de Voto, for instance) have of course stressed this Americanness, this non-literary quality, in their heroes; and scholarship about them still forms a separate current, a warm frothy Gulf Stream of positive thinking, in the critical ocean.

Then they had the gift, so rare among literary men, so necessary in public relations, for adopting in their own name the language of a group, a category; the group-language of the New York ferryboat men, the Broadway bus-drivers, the soldiers in hospital; or of the Nevada miners, the Mississippi river-pilots, the Connecticut businessmen; languages formed to express not the private self-definition of the speaker, but his public self-identification with the listeners. Whitman, for instance, was very successful in maintaining personal relationships on that level, with a good deal of emotion invested in them. He rather avoided relationships involving that other use of language, where narrowly defined meanings are dominant, and broadly unifying emotions are avoided. His personal style, in letters, is largely unformed. For him and for Twain, other people were a panorama of groups, types, trades, classes, rather than the dramas of self-discovery and self-salvation they were for – to take an extreme example – D. H. Lawrence, but also, in some degree, Emerson, Melville, Hawthorne.

Both were profoundly disorganised minds. They were strikingly incapable of organising a long piece of writing. They were incapable of a coherent attitude to a general topic, except where public opinion made that universal, as in the case of slavery after the war. They scarcely had coherent imaginative personalities. Twain's contradictory feelings about, for instance, Hannibal, and Whitman's about democracy, were not different aspects of a complexity, but unreconciled separate attitudes.

At the same time, no one presented to the world a more unified theatrical front. For all their seeming, and genuine, naïveté, they had highly sophisticated public personalities. They dressed to dramatise themselves; Twain in his white plantation-owner's suit, Whitman in his plebeian flannel shirt and broad-brimmed hat. They aimed at conspicuousness; Twain strolling down Fifth Avenue just as people came out of church on Sundays, Whitman writing from Boston, 'Of course I cannot walk through Washington Street (their Broadway here) without creating an immense sensation'. They wrote about themselves incessantly; not only in their major works, but for newspapers and magazines. They were interviewed, quoted, biographised, photographed (in the most arranged poses), painted, sculpted, sketched, more than any writers before them. Whitman wrote little articles about himself appearing anonymously or pseudonymously, describing his appearance and personality, and saying how much he was loved, and which shops had the best photographs of him for sale. And they played these rôles not only in their creative work and in newspaper interviews, but on at least two intermediate theatres; on the lecture platform and in private with disciples. We are accus-

tomed to speak knowingly of the artist's mask nowadays, and to imply that it is part of every writer's
normal apparatus; but what we find in Twain and
Whitman reminds us how private, how discreet, most
writers' gestures are. It is not to Yeats or Joyce we can
compare their public personas, but to Wild Bill
Hickock and Joaquin Miller. Their sense of a public,
an enormous, faceless, undiscriminating public, had
penetrated their private lives; their heights and depths
of emotion related to moments involving them and an
audience.

Reading Twain's accounts of his speech at the Grant
dinner (the height of joy) or the one for Emerson, Whittier, and Holmes (the depths of despair) you might think
this trait merely the result of his platform career, or of
the talent that embodied. But Whitman, who had
neither that career nor that talent, had the same temperament, the same radical showmanship. His love of
public performance is at the heart of his poetic inspiration. During the crucial years before 1855 he rode up
and down Broadway beside the drivers of buses, reciting
at the top of his voice into the mid-town din; and, as he
says, 'the influence of those Broadway omnibus jaunts
and drivers and declamations and escapades undoubted-
ly entered into the gestation of *Leaves of Grass*'.

Lastly, perhaps most important for our present
purposes, they were both easy liars. Whitman's
accounts of himself, for both general and private con-
sumption, were lavishly falsified; he wrote kind criticisms and bold defences of his own work under other
people's names; he wrote, for instance, an introductory
essay to his poems, and sent it to W. M. Rossetti,
assuring him that it was by William O'Connor. Richard
Chase says, 'At least he does not come bounding up to
us with that doglike guilelessness our contemporary
culture admires', but that does not soothe away our

sense of protest. Quite apart from who these doglike contemporaries might be (a fine example of the defensive red herring), we surely see Whitman paying the artistic price of this habitual duplicity in, for instance, 'Children of Adam'. Not that a serious writer has to be literally truthful, but he has to have a higher opinion of his reader's ability to detect a lie, a subtler conception of what a lie is, a subtler conception of his whole relationship as a writer to his reader. Whitman's conception was too like that of an advertiser to his public – or of Davy Crockett to his constituents.

Among Twain's reminiscences, some have been identified as not only lavishly fictionalised, but as having happened to other people in the first place. And he pays the artistic price in, for instance, 'The Private History of a Campaign that Failed'; where we are left saying, 'But how *did* it feel? Why did you join, what did you think at the time, why did you lose faith?' It obviously wasn't just funny at the time; nor could the men involved have been *that* simplistically boyish; he has given us a palpably false account. The same is true of the duels he got involved in in Nevada; what was such an experience like? Not that he need give us the literal, or even the sober, truth. But in his fantasy we expect to find some evidence that such an event did in fact happen to him – that he was *capable* of such an experience – because if he wasn't the story is in the crucial sense a lie.

We tend nowadays to imply that there are no limits to the amount of fabrication and suppression a writer can employ in turning his experience into a book; but in fact literature is closely related to truth-telling of a certain sort. The central problem of the 'American' heritage – of that mass of rich legend and language taken over by the writers of mid-nineteenth-century America – was its very different sense of the truth. There was a much broader sense of permissible gesture in all the great figures and legends of that tradition, and a much weaker interest in moral-psychological plausibility. There was a much louder, laxer, stagier relation between writer and reader. These gestures, these relationships, had produced the imaginative material the serious writers seized on, but they were at war with crucial literary criteria.

When Henry James was explaining why he had treated so little ' "unconventional" American life', he alleged the need to use the ugly local dialects, made ugly by a confusion between 'the speech of the soil and the speech of the newspaper'; however partial this anti-thesis, James certainly symbolises that faculty in the literary conscience which was thereby alienated from the 'American' material. It is because Twain and Whitman had so little of that faculty, had so odd a form of that conscience, that we are at so much of a loss when we read them nowadays.

Different as they are, we feel, if we read them honestly, that both are equally non-literary. This feeling takes the form, when we read Whitman, of anguished protests – 'You're making a fool of yourself – look what you're saying – this is exactly what you can't *do* in a poem'. In Twain's case, until we dismiss our literary expectations, it takes the form of a resentful impatience, 'Don't be so funny – don't be so charming – what did you really feel?'

Non-literary here refers of course to the major meanings of literary. Obviously Twain was one of the world's great artists in the minor meanings. Nobody ever used words more skilfully; he defined and achieved his purposes beautifully. But in the use of language to aesthetic effects, the most important surely involve the definition of truths of personal experience – personal here implying a self-responsible adult personality, whose reactions and discriminations are in some measure moral self-commitments, whose self-expression seeks the response of other such personalities. It is in this sense that Twain is not concerned with personal truth, and that therefore literary criteria do not apply themselves to his work. They do apply themselves to Whitman – because he so loudly offers to discuss personal truth – but they are hideously offended by what they find there. He is non-literary in the minor meanings of the word, too.

In Whitman's case the point is fairly easily made. The 'I' of 'Song of Myself' is first of all Walt Whitman, later all Americans, later the Unconscious or World Spirit; and though there is some humorous interplay of differentness between those selves, there is also a more remarkable indeterminate sliding from one into another. The self-responsible personality disappears. The crucial distinction, between what the poet felt, and what he might have felt if he had been somebody else, is fatally blurred; and this blurring extends to his tone as well as to his vision. He is not speaking *to* any more than *as* a person. The social situation he sets up with his readers is always tending to become that of a speaker before a huge shapeless crowd, highly excitable and responsive and uncritical, each of whom he has to merge with himself, and with each other. There are no satisfactory persons in Whitman's poetic world, neither the 'I' nor the 'You', and consequently there is no satisfaction in it for the reader.

Despite Whitman's official reputation, many literary people will grant this argument fairly easily. The difficulty is to make the opposite point, that Whitman remains an important writer.

This is not just because of the fragments of successful poetry that are scattered through *Leaves of Grass*.

Richard Chase has put the case for them very ably in *Walt Whitman Reconsidered*; one would add only that Whitman is also, from time to time, a very poignant poet of sexual provocation.

‘ Ever the old inexplicable query, ever that thorn'd thumb, that
     breath of itches and thirsts,
Ever the vexer's hoot, hoot, till we find where the sly one hides
     and bring him forth,
Ever love, ever the sobbing liquid of life,
Ever the bandage under the chin, ever the trestle of death.   ’

And in another piece, after a reference to the 'guile, anger, lust, hot wishes I dared not speak', he continues,

‘ Was called by my nighest name by clear loud voices of young
     men, as they saw me approaching or passing,
Felt their arms on my neck as I stood, or the negligent leaning of
     their flesh against me as I sat,
Saw many I loved in the street or ferry-boat or public assembly,
     yet never told them a word,
Lived the same life with the rest, the same laughing, gnawing,
     sleeping,
Play'd the part that still looks back on the actor or actress,
The same old rôle, the rôle that is what we make it, as great as
     we like,
Or as small as we like, or both great and small.   ’

There are such moments, but they are always succeeded, or interfused, with something so much the opposite that it remains an essentially painful experience to read *Leaves of Grass* with one's literary sensibility aroused. ('I dote on myself, there is that lot of me and all so luscious' may serve as a sufficient reminder of all that is referred to.) Whitman is not only non-literary, he is anti-literary. He offers to discuss personal experience, and then forces on us everything but that – catalogues of objects, political exhortations, ideas of sexuality, day-dreams, grotesque posturings. Even his catalogues are of things he had read about, not seen and heard himself. In a word, he does not tell us the truth. Quite often, he tells lies; he says he has felt and seen things which he has not. Again and again, he makes a fool of himself; having invited us into his mind, with our keenest expectations aroused, he appears before us in a tatty series of road company spangles, cutting capers he's never properly practised. And all the time he asks his readers to cease to be persons (people who respect their own emotions, who commit themselves in a reaction only when that further extends and defines their personality in new and risky areas of experience) and to become partisans, members of a crowd, merging with each other in a stock response. In reading Whitman, therefore, despite moments of pleasure, a reader has to force himself, to go against his nature as reader.

In *not* reading Whitman, however, an intelligent man also makes an unnatural sacrifice. Not for the fragments of successful poetry, but for the outline of a significant literary venture that everywhere comes through when you read sympathetically. Whitman confronted the ideas of his time, some of its crucial experience, its poetic theory, its language, and strove to make something large out of them. He failed atrociously in nine-tenths of his particular effects, but his general intention, coming dimly through, engages our interest. One can understand why he was a source for better poets, and very different ones, coming after him. But we can only respond to that intention, act on that interest, if we switch off the spotlight of critical awareness – the crucial component in any literary discipline – and work in the penumbra of a general humanism; a general interest in intellectual history, aesthetic theory and so on. It is because it is so hard for literary critics to do this, and because Whitman must, as time goes by, become more and more their property, that he is generally neglected today. With rare exceptions like Mr Chase, he has been abandoned to the obscurity of an official reputation; and so long as literary study retains its rigour, this is perhaps the kindest fate that can befall him, unjust though it is. The solution to the problem of 'American' literature has in his case been oblivion.

When we come to Twain, the problem is complicated by the case of *Huckleberry Finn*. Modern critics have decided more or less unanimously that this is a great novel – there is only controversy over whether or not it is 'perfect' – and have therefore found in it all kinds of personal truth. F. R. Leavis, T. S. Eliot, and Lionel Trilling have all made the largest claims for it as a great book – perhaps the greatest book in American literature: naturally a dozen less well-known critics have followed them; and Twain is established among the supreme artists. I shall claim that this is a clear, and colossal, case of misreading, but the quarrel is too long to be sandwiched into this present argument – it has a later section to itself.

Assuming that point made (that *Huckleberry Finn* is the same kind of book as, say, *Tom Sawyer*) we would conclude that Twain's talents (which were certainly brilliant) were primarily those of a great humorist. Following his own definition, we can distinguish that from a great wit, or a great comic writer. The humorous story, he said, differed from a witty or comic story, in that it depended entirely on the manner of the narrator and not at all on his matter. Indeed, it is striking how entirely without point are stories like 'Jim Baker and the Bluejays' or 'The Jumping Frog'. The whole effect depends on your continuing awareness of the narrator – not as a satiric intelligence, but as an artful performer. The whole experience consists of events occurring to that sense. Your attention is concentrated on the entertainer, on his phrasing and pace, on the tricks he will play on you; and his attention is concentrated on you, or rather on the audience as a whole; no one is deeply aware of the events he is narrating, or of the moral or sentimental idea behind them, both of which he is palpably manipulating for his own purposes. Genial though he is, he does not allow anything to distract you for long from your duty towards him as performer, entertainer, star.

It is in this sense, that he turns his reader into one of a group, that Twain resembles Whitman. The reader is not here one of a crowd, all loving and hating together, but he is one of an audience, laughing and crying together. His reaction is again not self-commitment, but participation in a group-emotion. This is in fact truer of Twain than of other humorous writers. The platform humorists – Josh Billings, Artemus Ward, Orpheus C. Kerr – of whom Twain was the greatest – all used the milder and less risky parts of the Frontier tradition of humour. Huck Finn is a much less disturbing character than Sut Lovingood (who has sexual experience, is capable of violence, is capable of self-hatred) and the humour Twain builds round Huck is less challenging than George Washington Harris's. Twain worked hard not to offend, and his effects were calculated to give the greatest happiness to the greatest number; no challenge is made to the reader's judgement, no self-committing response is demanded; you react merely as one of an audience.

It is true that Twain sometimes offered his audience the reverse of entertainment – in *The Mysterious Stranger*, for example. And it is true that in some sense he always felt constrained, writing as he did, and often tried to be something more than a humorist. But whenever he stepped markedly outside that rôle, his work lost in authority. Twain's melancholy and pessimism are among the traits that make us see him as a journalistic rather than a serious writer. He had that typical consciousness of having slightly falsified, slightly sweetened everything, to make it generally palatable; he had accumulated over years the sense that if he ever spoke out all he thought it would not only make him hated, but would drive other men to suicide; but when he did speak out there was nothing there but loud cynicism and bad philosophy. His talents – for observation, for mimicry, for irony – came to life only when he was entertaining.

In the humorous tale, events and characters and settings are not deeply realised – no intensity of awareness is directed at them. On the whole, this remained true of Twain's work even when he was writing full-length novels; it is when we return from the dramatic action or the long speech to the central voice that we feel in the hands of a great master again, and at the heart of the aesthetic experience. But there are important exceptions to this because, in ways that transcend the limits of humour, Twain was a fine lyric poet, a master of spoken language ·in print, and a beautiful ironist.

The first two talents are best exemplified in *Huckleberry Finn*, but the third becomes major in *A Connecticut Yankee*; and this book represents Twain's true achievement perhaps better than the more famous one. It is not of course the satire on sixth-century England which is exciting, though it is honest and vigorous, and has its own effectiveness in its place. But Twain is not aware of half the ways of feeling about the past which are available to us. His understanding of that society, and history in general, is not rich enough. He sets up his Aunt Sallies, and knocks them down again, without once involving us, without stimulating us to a new awareness of either the past or the present.

Nor is it, as some modern critics say, that the nightmare ending gives dignity to the whole book retroactively, by proving that Twain did after all hate the nineteenth century. Twain did not hate the nineteenth century; those chapters do not affect the meaning of the rest of the book; and they are of no literary interest. Twain was writing out of some private fantasy there, and though that was no doubt related to a very deep self-distrust ('What a man sees in the human race is merely himself in the deep and honest privacy of his own heart. Byron despised the race because he despised himself. I feel as Byron did and for the same reasons.') that whole area of his experience never engaged his major talents, never expressed itself successfully.

The important part of the book is the friendly, uncritical, but lively irony it directs at the Yankee himself and what he stands for. This amounts to one of the fullest renderings of and comments on the nineteenth-century mind at its briskest. The method is simply to isolate and intensify the most self-confident tones of a nineteenth-century voice, against the implicit background of, not any opposing attitude, or criticism, or any philosophical largeness, but simply the more self-doubtful tones of the same voice. It is given the amused attention one might give a younger and more energetic brother. Contemporary readers were shown the extreme towards which their world was tending, but wholly from within – for laughter, not alarm.

‘ I made up my mind to two things; if it was still the 19th century and I was among lunatics and couldn't get away, I would presently boss that asylum or know the reason why; and if on the other hand it was really the 6th century, all right, I didn't want any softer thing. I would boss the whole country inside of three months; for I judged I would have the start of the best-educated man in the kingdom by a matter of thirteen hundred years or upwards. I'm not a man to waste time after my mind's made up and there's work on hand; so I said. . . . *'*

Even in that passage you can see what pungency is being given to the word boss; Sir Boss is the title the Yankee chooses when he acquires power in Camelot, and the book as a whole gives the word its definitive personality in English. The energetic levelling down of everything (equalising the nineteenth-century asylum and the sixth-century kingdom) is dramatised by the perfectly authentic rhythms and vocabulary. 'Know the reason why' and 'by a matter of' and 'any softer thing', and the way the sentence turns its corner round 'all right'; all this brings the sound and feel of the voice inside the reader; and dramatises the 'point' without the least exaggeration or falsification.

As irony this is as superior to any in *Huckleberry Finn* as Bob Hope is a better comedian than Bing Crosby (Crosby was given the part of the Yankee when they made a film of the book); because it is based on an energetic, self-respecting, conscious cleverness, instead of on a flaccid and vacuous self-conscious charm. The satirical elements (in the ironical parts – not the Carlylean pictures of social degradation) are as superior to the satire of the other novel as the real king, Arthur, is to the fake King. (There is so much of the fake King – the sordidness and violence – which Twain can't deal with.) The philistinism, for instance, which seems to shock so many critics, is quite masterly.

' Raphael was a bird. We had several of his chromos; one was his "Miraculous Draught of Fishes", where he puts in a miracle of his own – puts three men into a canoe which wouldn't have held a dog without upsetting. I always admired to study R's art, it was so fresh and unconventional. *'*

What a wonderful tone he gives to words like chromo and bird; how miracle shrivels at the edges in that company; what zest in the whole passage. This is not of course straight philistinism; but much less is it a satire on philistinism; the sauce is partly a delight in the impudence of this particular attitude, partly the general delight in being a humorist. It does not withdraw any of the outrageousness; it merely draws humorous attention to it. 'There did not seem to be brains enough in the entire nursery, so to speak, to bait a fish-hook with.'

This is a more interesting voice than Huck's because of the Yankee's great social reality, but also because there is much more of Twain's own temperament and experience in it. The Yankee is a conscious showman: 'Ah, he fetched them; it was a rattling good stroke', and 'I couldn't have played it better myself', occur all the way through; and since this trait is implicit in Twain's voice at all times, the book gains immensely in psychological reality – Huck, so far as we can believe in him at all, could never have written half the passages attributed to him. For this reason, no doubt, the elaborate contrivances of the Valley of Holiness are better than anything similar in the other book (with the possible exception of the faking of Huck's own suicide). Also this is the voice of Twain, the full thriving member of nineteenth-century city society; the common sense, the scorn for the past, the delight in his own cleverness, the Robinson Crusoe ambition, they are all in *Huckleberry Finn* too, but there they have to be romanticised, whereas in this book they are frankly admitted and exactly rendered. It is a surprisingly full portrait. For instance, the narrator is, he says, a Yankee; 'and therefore practical; and nearly barren of sentiment, I suppose – poetry, in other words'. In fact, of course, he is full of sentiment; it is only emotion he refuses.

And Twain in effect – in aesthetic effect – tells us as much. 'At length, out of the silence a noble Latin chant – men's voices – broke and swelled up and rolled away into the night, a majestic tide of melody. I had put that up, too, and it was one of the best effects I ever invented.' He shows us the dry, quick, self-minimising voice imposing itself on the larger experience. It is at moments like this that Twain comes closest to moral complexity.

But on the whole this is of course an entertainment rather than a novel. The writer is not concerned to define truths of personal experience, and if we read it with any major literary expectations, we shall be disappointed. It is a brilliant piece of writing of a minor kind. The opposite of Whitman, Twain deserves our attention not for what he attempts without success, but for what he achieves in despite of his aims. Exactly like Whitman, however, he engages our attention as humanists rather than as literary critics. To bear down upon him with the apparatus we reserve for major novelists is to hypertrophy and fictionalise that attention.

It is however easy to see the temptation to treat *Huckleberry Finn* that way. We find in it some of the most beautiful writing in the American language, as accurate and vivid as that of *A Connecticut Yankee*, and much richer in its pastoral and romantic tones. This occurs in the chapters that describe the life on the raft when Jim and Huck are alone together, and more generally in passages where Huck is in direct contact with Nature, or in which he has simple adventures, or in which he is recording objects. The freshness of feeling there combines with a classic simplicity to give the impression of a major talent under perfect control; to meet, on the very next page, signs of the crudest faking of the whole literary enterprise, naturally baffles; it is easier to re-interpret the signs than to accept the paradox. Moreover, the epic shape of the book, made effulgent by the wonderfully rendered experience of floating down the river, releases a thousand hints that the largest meanings are involved, a thousand invitations to organise adult moral experience into the book's symbolic shapes. But Twain in effect rescinds all those invitations.

The life on the raft, for instance, does not represent freedom in any of the interesting senses of that word. It is a purely lazy, relaxed, floating-down-the-river freedom, categorically on holiday, categorically an escape from all responsibility. Twain is very insistent about this. It is not freedom to do anything; it is not even freedom *from* anything important. It is freedom from table-manners and formal clothes, and evening prayers. It is absolutely illegitimate to read this as a quarrel with society, or an aspiration, however vague, to some other mode of being, when Twain insists that it is self-indulgence; a non-serious yearning for some relaxation of those disciplines which (again Twain *insists*) are absolutely necessary.

> ‘Two months or more run along, and my clothes got to be all rags, and dirt, and I didn't see how I'd ever got to like it so well at the widow's, where you had to wash and eat on a plate, and comb up, and go to bed and get up regular, and be for ever bothering over a book and have old Miss Watson pecking at you all the time. I didn't want to go back no more. I had stopped cussing, because the widow didn't like it; but now I took to it again because pap hadn't no objections.’

The succession of details amounts to a perfectly clear statement by Twain that if you aren't disciplined you lose your respectability, and if you lose your respectability you become sordid.

Twain is in fact much less available to 'interpretation' than most writers; both because he was so skilful, directing our responses so exactly, and because he was so timid, avoiding crucial personal experience as subject matter. The only times he surrenders to his subject are when he writes out of his fantasy life, and there is less of that in this novel than in *A Connecticut Yankee*.

Twain gives us a hundred notices that this is not a highly organised book, in which there will be significant parallels, inversions, extensions of meaning between the episodes, but a loosely strung series of set-pieces, each of which is to be read for itself. The chapter subheadings are one kind of such notice. 'Hamlet's Soliloquy – A Shakespearean Revival – Loafing Around Town – Old Boggs – Death of Boggs.' Each of these is an exercise in a well-known mode, perfectly fulfils itself as such, and does not exist in any other sense. To think about Jim's deaf child outside the anecdote in which she appears is exactly as perverse as to ask how many children Lady Macbeth had. The form of the books tells us that, too; its series of episodes, that it is about a child, that it is written for children, that this boy is running away from civilisation, that at the end he wants to run away again – all this, which is now credited with such portentous meanings for American culture, is itself the guarantee that all those meanings are illusory.

Those critics who find the book 'subversive' and 'revolutionary' believe that, despite all these directions to the reader, Twain nevertheless packed into the book some intensely imagined material of an opposite tendency. But surely we must consult the criteria of quality in our estimate of intensity, and surely all the best writing in the book is in the mode of relaxation and playfulness. The scene of the attempted lynching, for instance, and Colonel Sherburn's speech, have nothing like the authority of the scenes of life on the raft. The social melodrama at its very best (Pap's delirium tremens, for example) can only remind us of Dickens, and how much more vivid Dickens makes that sort of thing. And the cynicism of, for instance, the two men who refuse to help Huck when he tells them his father has smallpox, and then tell him how to fool other people into helping him; this is the low-toned, prudential cynicism of common conversation. There is no concentration of imagination, no investment of emotion, there; it is rather an insurance against imaginative and emotional involvement. There is no invitation in any such writing to seek a meaning for the whole book, no warrant to disregard Twain's general directions for reading, no interesting – however fragmentary – judgement on experience.

It is therefore not possible, for instance, to read a significant parallel between the deafness of Jim's daughter in his anecdote in chapter 23, and the mock deafness of the Duke in chapter 24.* Each deafness has its point, the first pathetic, the second farcical, and its meaning is completed there. To bear in mind the first deafness when we come to the second is to do violence to the text, to refuse to respond as the author is directing.

‘ Then he turns around, blubbering, and makes a lot of idiotic signs to the duke on his hands, and blamed if *he* didn't drop a carpet-bag and bust out a-crying. If they warn't the beatenest lot, them two frauds, that ever I struck.

Well, the men gathered around, and sympathized with them, and said all sorts of kind things to them, and carried their carpet-bags up the hill for them, and let them lean on them and cry, and told the king all about his brother's last moments, and the king he told it all over again on his hands to the duke, and both of

* This, and the idea discussed in the next paragraph, are typical examples of contemporary readings of the book.

The critics who read that last sentence literally, as bitter and judgemental, are doing violence to the text. Twain is asking us to find the incident simply funny. There *is* a secondary meaning there which is somewhat in conflict with the book's superficial ethic – Twain's anarchic sympathy with the King and the Duke, his delight in this mockery of human grief – but this is purely secondary. Neither here, nor anywhere else in the book, does this kind of effect have the imaginative weight behind it that it has in, say, Evelyn Waugh.

Nor is it possible to read a significant parallel between the literary world of the adults and that of the children (signifying that all society is founded on illusion, on story-books) in the early chapters. Each little anecdote there, the widow and her bible stories, Tom Sawyer and his pirate books, has its point clearly defined, and its purpose amply fulfilled. Each is aimed at a well-marked area of conventional humour, and when it has been responded to that way it ceases to exist. Twain forbids us to keep it in mind as 'real' in any sense. We are not even allowed to ask where Jim is during the Wilks episode, or what happened to the Huck-Jim relationship during the book's final chapters.

The only constant, connecting reality is the writer. Not Huck himself. Huck sinks to being a mere recorder quite often, and occasionally disappears. For instance,

' The undertaker never got in ahead of Emmeline but once, and then she hung fire on a rhyme for the dead person's name, which was Whistler. She warn't ever the same after that: she never complained but she kind of pined away and did not live long. '

This is Twain writing, not Huck; the phrasing is that of a conscious performer. Indeed the whole section on the Grangerfords, which is made up of two or three quite separate set-pieces, can only be read as a unity if you refer constantly back to the great entertainer who is offering you one piece after another out of his repertoire. The last person who could have written it is naïve, literal-minded, innocent-eyed Huck Finn. In fact, whenever a comic point can be made at the cost of some plausibility in Huck, the latter is sacrificed. 'I was most ready to cry' when he might be excluded from Tom's robber gang; and they decided 'we would all go home and meet next week and rob somebody and kill some people'. These are exactly the terms the naïve mind would avoid, could not afford to use, because they explode the illusion.

But above all, where Huck does exist, it is as a narrative voice (a wonderfully fresh and flexible one) not as a full personality. The obvious contrast is Salinger's Holden Caulfield. Huck has no moral experience, no full relationships, no physique, no psychological type, no social personality, no sexuality, no violence, no impulses but a purely conventional mischief, curiosity, timidity.

When Huck 'thinks' about, for instance, slavery, every detail is aimed directly at the reader's settled convictions, to evoke an easy laughter and renewed complacency. There is no attempt to render, much less provoke, a genuine debate in a genuine mind.

'It most froze me to hear such talk. He wouldn't ever dared to talk such talk in his life before. Just see what a difference it made in him the minute he judged he was about free. It was according to the old saying, "Give a nigger an inch, and he'll take an ell". Thinks I, this is what comes of my not thinking. Here was this nigger which I had as good as helped to run away, coming right out flat-footed and saying he would steal his children – children that

> belonged to a man I didn't even know; a man who hadn't ever
> done me no harm.

Both vocabulary and constructions ('It most froze me
– he wouldn't ever dared – just see – it was according
to the old saying') tell us not to take the debate seriously; in fact, the voice Twain is imitating there is
not Huck's at all, but the proverbial old woman's. Then
the great nineteenth-century words 'free' and 'children'
and 'belonged' release a flood of stock response, and
sweep along any more risky, individualised feelings a
reader might have for himself – Twain certainly didn't
evoke any – into canalised audience appreciation.

The book's liveliest moral moments occur, not in
passages like this, but in, for instance, the story of the
undertaker at the Wilks' funeral; with his 'kind of
coarse whisper' and 'He had a rat'; it is there, with no
large principles in view, that Twain's moral analysis
is at its most acute, subtle, lively; when it is at the
service of his most playful wit. The 'debates' in Huck's
mind on 'serious issues' are wholly two-dimensional.

> "Is your man black or white?"
> I didn't answer up prompt. I tried to, but the words wouldn't
> come. I tried for a second or two, to brace up and out with it,
> but I warn't man enough – hadn't the spunk of a rabbit. I see I
> was weakening; so I just gave up trying, and up and says, "He's
> white".

The tension is wholly external, in our wanting him to
say white; the point is wholly in his sense of the wrong
answer being our sense of the right one. We never enter
his mind; nor do we ever ask ourselves what else the
answer should – *could*, morally – be. The moral terms
are absolutely simple.

And if Huck is not a person, much less is Jim. It is
a fairly frequent claim for the book that here we have

the first fully real Negro in literature, but in point of fact, Jim is straight out of the Christy's minstrels, by way of Uncle Tom's Cabin. He talks to himself, refers to himself as 'Jim', exaggerates and interprets dreams and omens, his superstitions and ignorances are all comic, his virtues and qualities all the stock Christian pathos and passivity, the stock warm animal comradeship, of the stock Negro. He is well done, but he is as conventional as can be.

As for the realism with which the book is credited – which it is said to have invented – that is the most puzzling of all. We are asked to believe that Huck and Jim called the King 'your majesty' all the weeks they were with him on the raft, and went down on one knee to speak to him, and did not sit down in his presence until he asked them to. Obviously this is not a realism that puts any stress on the plausibility of events. Nor is it a plausibility of the narrative manner, as the Emmeline Grangerford episode demonstrates. Nor is it an unsentimental honesty in Huck's responses to events and people, when he describes them as 'the sweetest old grey-headed lady' and 'he straightened himself up like a liberty-pole, and the lightning began to flicker out from under his eyebrows'.

One can only guess that the book's 'realism' is a policy of relying on only one's simplest relationships – with objects and sensations – and suspending one's response in all more complex involvements, with individuals and society. This can be found in Huck (though Twain did not put it there); and in the hands of, say, Hemingway, when combined with the imitation of spoken language, it becomes something with which the word 'realism' can be associated. For Twain's book, 'realistic' is about the least appropriate of all labels.

Huckleberry Finn is a charming children's book, with some beautiful passages, but the significant novel by that name which contemporary critics discuss does not exist. Nor does the novelist to whom they give the name Mark Twain. Both were invented; to body forth the critics' idea of a great novel, and to rescue such a rich talent from such poverty of meaning.

Twain and Whitman together, the entertainer and the prophet, amply represent 'American' literature, and the problems that it poses the modern reader. All those books inherited something of the Frontier tradition's alienation from conventional literature, its rejection of finicky discriminations, its attempt at a larger, coarser vitality. Twain and Whitman in particular inherited that tradition's bolder and stagier relation to its audience; its avoidance of personal experience as subject matter, its deprecation of personal scrutiny in the reader. As such they affront the literary reader in his very soul. And yet they remain an important part of literary history. They have to be read. But that reading can be both sympathetic and honest only after a masking of the crucial critical faculty, only in the mellower light of a generalised literary-historical-philosophical sensibility – the sensibility of humanism. Modern criticism has so far failed to make this sacrifice; it has cut the Gordian knot by denying Whitman the kind of interest he has, and awarding Twain the kind he has not.

Henry James

and the Great Tradition

‘ He is, all the same, one of the great. His registration of sophisticated human consciousness is one of the classical creative
achievements; it *added* something as only genius can. And when
he is at his best that something is seen to be of great human
significance. He creates an ideal civilised sensibility; a humanity
capable of communicating by the finest shades of inflection and
implication; a nuance may engage a whole complex moral
economy and the perceptive response be the index of a major
valuation or choice. ’

F. R. Leavis: *The Great Tradition*

This statement deserves the closest attention, and not
only for its source; it articulates the implicit claim of
James's other admirers, and it crystallises the problem
for the rest of the world. There can be no question that
James was a brilliant novelist; but there can be argument about whether he deserves the attentiveness and
suggestibility we yield up to writers when we call them
‘great’. Of course he has ‘added something’ for his
admirers; that effect, after all, is simply the result of
their admiration, their intense attentiveness, their inner
submission. The rest of us can still question his greatness and their exposition of it; both for artistic failures
in the novels which embody this ‘ideal civilised sensibility’, and for poverties of human understanding which

seem to go along with it; and also for the nature of his influence on his admirers – for the Jamesian sensibility we see at work in others – just *for* what he 'added'. This is why Dr Leavis's statement is so valuable. He brings into focus, as so often, exactly the point of view from which the problem is most interesting. It is the idea that James changed the spectrum of feeling – that all educated men must now see life, to an important degree, the way James saw it – that some of us cannot accept.

We can begin by noting an aspect of James's work which is not much discussed by the critics, but which is one of its most vivid features for me. This is a kind of comedy so self-consciously clever that it defeats its own object; the reader finds himself, to put it crudely, laughing at the writer as well as with him. For instance, in *The Awkward Age* –

> "Oh, Nanda, she's my best friend after three or four others."
>
> "After so many?" Mr Longdon laughed. "Don't you think that's rather a back seat, as they say, for one's best?"
>
> "A back seat?" she wondered with a purity!
>
> "If you don't understand," said her companion, "it serves me right, as your aunt didn't leave me with you to teach you the slang of the day."
>
> "The slang?" she again spotlessly speculated.
>
> "You've never even heard the expression? I should think that a great compliment to our time if it weren't that I fear it may have been only the name that has been kept from you."
>
> The light of ignorance in the child's smile was positively golden. "The name?" she again echoed.

It is inexact to say that the reader laughs at the writer here, because even his bizarrest effects do not have the crudity of lapses; they are rather perfections, refinements, continuous with the whole accomplished performance; their effect is to check our general participation, our co-operative assent, turning that into a baffled reassessment of the writer's intention.

The Awkward Age is however written in the late style, and James's admirers concede an over-cleverness in that last part of his career. Since the purpose of this essay is to challenge the current estimate, it would be a waste of time to demonstrate a failure where no one claimed a success; I shall not discuss any but those works which are praised by the best critics, in which they find his genius at work. *The Awkward Age* is one of those; but to show that this aspect of the novel is not a blemish deriving just from those late vices, let us take some examples from earlier work. For instance, in *Washington Square*, 1881, there occurs this little passage:

' "Be so good as to let me know what is going on in the house", he said to her, in a tone which, under the circumstances, he himself deemed genial.

"Going on, Austin?" Mrs Penniman exclaimed, "Why, I am sure I don't know! I believe that last night the old grey cat had kittens!"

"At her age?" said the Doctor, "the idea is startling – almost shocking. Be so good as to see that they are all drowned. But what else has happened?"

"Ah, the dear little kittens!" cried Mrs Penniman, "I wouldn't have them drowned for the world."   '

For a moment the comedy perceptibly achieves a poise, a momentum, which makes it self-sustaining, and releases it from the burden of meaning – from the moral preoccupations of the fable as a whole. This is a very momentary effect, but similar ones recur throughout the novel; the treatment of the heroine is always verging on this, and the serious meaning suffers thereby.

' Catherine was immensely struck with this conception of the affair, which seemed eminently worthy of her lover's brilliant intellect; though she viewed it askance in so far as it depended upon her own powers of execution. The idea of being "clever" in a gondola by moonlight appeared to her to include elements of which her grasp was not active.   ,

Such language is so self-consciously exquisite it invites us to contemplate the heroine from a greater distance, and with a greater condescension, than we or the author can afford. It is a dandyism of style, incompatible with any real reverence before the dowdier human virtues which the novel is specially celebrating.

My last example is from *The Europeans*, 1878.

6   "Have you ever entertained the idea of settling in the United States?" he asked one morning, while Felix brilliantly plied his brush.

"My dear uncle," said Felix, "excuse me if your question makes me smile a little. To begin with, I have never entertained an idea. Ideas often entertain me; but I'm afraid I have never seriously made a plan. I know what you are going to say – or rather I know what you think, for I don't think that you will say it – that this is very frivolous and loose-minded on my part. So it is; but I am made like that; I take things as they come, and somehow there is always some new thing to follow the last. In the second place, I should never propose to *settle*. I can't settle, my dear uncle; I am not a settler."   ,

Once again we feel the self-conscious excitement of a style running away with itself, running away from the serious meaning the writer has proposed to treat; a cleverness not wholly engaged in its subject, and skidding slightly on its surface. And this time it seems to me one recognises the general class to which this kind of writing belongs; one recognises a likeness between James here and a very different writer. Isn't this moment like one in a scene by Oscar Wilde? Isn't this the same formality, theatricality, self-consciousness, thinness? Isn't there something of Wilde in all the examples – in the dialogue from *Washington Square*? Doesn't our bafflement with the first passage express a nascent doubt that we should be reading it the way we read *The Importance of Being Earnest*?

James is clearly, it seems to me, a contributor to that post-Victorian mode of dandyism-cum-nonsense, with its reflections in Carroll and Lear and its modern apotheosis in Evelyn Waugh. But this contribution is only an extreme case of tendencies in him which are very widespread, and which effectively deny him the kind of greatness ascribed.

Perhaps we can sum up these tendencies by saying that James aspired too insistently to both worldliness of tone and brilliancy of technique; and that even at his best these aspirations constantly threaten to become inappropriate and unconvincing. From time to time, as we have seen, they produce purely comic effects, and always they thin down the body of meaning communicated.

In a sense, of course, James is always worldly, and I wouldn't want to describe the general manner of, say, *The Portrait of a Lady*, as anything but beautifully achieved. But there are moments, even there, where one feels a straining after *savoir-faire*, a baseless sophistication. Ralph Touchett, for instance, is presented as exceptionally knowing, in a perfectly admirable way; in his understanding of personal motives, his knowledge of social manners, his aloofness from ordinary passions, his laughing evasion of straightforward questions. James has a lot invested in this character; who holds, as the example of 'good' sophistication, a key position in the architecture of the book; but who does not sustain it. Ralph is often offensive in his evasions, vulgar in his knowingness. When he hears that Henrietta and Isabel are going to London by themselves, he declares himself very much amused; meaning that they should not do it. He suggests he should have them 'put down' for his club. When Isabel protests, saying Henrietta can find her way about cities with safety and propriety, 'Ah,' said Ralph, 'let me take advantage of her protection to go up to town as well. I may never have a chance to travel so safely.' There is a disrespect for both the others here; not so much in the over-insistence on the proprieties as in the over-jocularity of the tone. Later he mistakes the dry, honourable directness of Henrietta's manner for a vulgar flirtatiousness; and is ready to suspect Isabel of having lied to him about dining alone in London. But James offers us this character for our moral admiration; and those for whom James is 'one of the great' accept him as he is offered.

Leavis says, of the worst of these episodes:

> Ralph's "lapse" doesn't matter. It merely leads us to say that he knows how to treat Henrietta, just as he knows how to treat everyone. For Ralph Touchett is the centre, the key-figure, of James's "system" − the poise of harmony I have spoken of as characterising *The Portrait of a Lady* ... He represents the ideal civilisation that James found in no country.

This is a striking example of the way James changes his admirers' sensibility, 'adds' something; for one can only call this knowing how to treat Henrietta if one shares James's view of her as radically absurd, greatly inferior to, say, Ralph himself, not fully human beside, say, Madame Merle. This is surely not a view that can recommend itself to others (I find Henrietta the most attractive of the three, in many ways) or recommend the general Jamesian sensibility. At its best it implies a scheme of values according to which impropriety of manner always speaks louder than honesty of heart at first, and a great volume of experience is required before that contrast can be reversed.

Ralph's 'ideal civilisation' is unconvincing; he is too cautious, too insistent on the proprieties and conventions, too ready to make feeble jokes at awkward moments; and it is inappropriate; his manner, at its best, is not an important enough thing to counterbalance the forces of death and love and evil which the book also invokes. Something similar is true in many of James's books. In *The Awkward Age* there is something flimsy, in the most worldly sense, in his brilliant group; they would not be very formidable, on their own ground; confronted with them, one could appeal to criteria by which they would appear small. They talk about sophistication and moral freedom much more than they achieve it. And consequently (this is the inappropriateness) the reader loses interest in the quality they are supposed to represent. Another example is Felix and Eugenia in *The Europeans*. They imply volumes of moral freedom every time they open their mouths; one gets so eager to know just what they would *do* that one is quite contemptuous of the actual flirtations and intrigues; but the point is that real worldliness does not insist so, just as real manners are less obtrusive, and real charm less loud. Not that the characters are just badly represented; we can believe in these traits, too, but with a different interpretation from the one James offered. Felix and Eugenia are perhaps *not* European, after all; they are Americans; they have the *religion* of Europe; and Gertrude will be another such – she is a zealot for frivolity, neurotically nonchalant. The scenes James presents answer to this interpretation vividly; but his comments insist on the opposite; Felix and Eugenia are the fine flowers of a rich civilisation – Eugenia a little too much of one – and as unselfconscious about it as flowers expanding in sunshine.

The point has been made that James did not in fact

know the best people, and that this is evident in his writing. One can sometimes think, reading stories like 'The Marriages' and 'The Death of the Lion', that he didn't know anybody. His versions of British social life are often wildly improbable, derived from contemporary melodrama; and he is never a notable observer. Let us take, as a last example, 'The Beldonald Holbein', a story describing how an old lady gets invited to parties because she looks like a painting.

> ‘... the hurrying and the nudging and the pressing and the staring; see the people "making up" and introduced, and catch the word when they have had their turn; hear it, above all, the great one, "Ah, yes, the famous Holbein".’

Does this render first-hand experience of social life? James does not handle 'the world' really well; nor the 'worldly' tone; one feels he was fascinated and over-awed by both. Not of course in the most vulgar sense. James certainly was seeking an ideal civilisation, and making use of the real only to that purpose. But his imagination was not bold enough. His ideal (Ralph) was too much like the real; his own tone is too much like ordinary worldliness; insecurely imitative of that. He attempted a sophisticated manner in and out of season, and too often this makes him seem provincial, and even vulgar, gaping at the spectacle of other people's stylishness when they deserve no attention.

Determined as he was to be worldly, James was equally eager to be technically brilliant. It is the inter-action of these two ambitions, which, when poorly controlled, produces those passing likenesses to Oscar Wilde. He bears down so hard on his material, makes it so much a field for the display of his talent, that the reader is turned from participant to spectator. For instance, his descriptions are liable to break up the object into a series of sense-impressions which are linked together more by verbal values, alliteration, rhythm, rhyme, than by their real life interrelations.

'. . . past cottages thatched and timbered, past ale-houses latticed and sanded, past patches of ancient common and glimpses of empty parks, between hedgerows made thick by midsummer. '

The effect is to reduce the scene to a backdrop, to something the writer has thrown together for the moment. The diminution of reality is more striking, becomes dismissal, where he feels some uneasiness with the thing described.

'Six months later however I was favoured with a visit from an elderly dreary dingy person who introduced herself to me as Mr Brooksmith's aunt . . . The room into which I was shown was above the small establishment of a dyer and cleaner who had inflated kid gloves and discoloured shawls in his shop-front. There was a great deal of grimy infant life up and down the place, and there was a hot moist smell within, as of the "boiling" of dirty linen. '

Sometimes the effect is less purely verbal (in this next example James is imitating a painter) and the intention is to glorify the thing seen; but the effect is still to break it up into units at the artist's disposal and to diminish its independent reality:

'. . . a stout grey pile, of the softest, deepest, most weather-fretted hue, rising from a broad, still, moat, it seemed to Isabel a castle in a fairy-tale . . . the watery sunshine rested on the walls in blurred and desultory gleams, washing them, as it were, in places tenderly chosen, where the ache of antiquity was keenest. '

The same thing can be found in both characterisation and plot. In the latter I will mention only the over-symmetry and the over-use of confidantes. *What Maisie*

Knew may stand as the type-case of the first, and *The Ambassadors* of the second. One is always being reminded of the skill with which the narrative is being handled, with an insistence which is in effect clumsy; since, like the descriptive passages quoted, these effects reduce the reader's rôle to that of passive spectator, and the characters to puppets. They also produce simple mistakes. For instance, in *The Bostonians*, James's florid gestures of technical skill (he brings his characters on and off like a ringmaster in a circus) leads him to give Olive Chancellor a psychologically wrong first speech. Mrs Luna has remarked that Olive never goes through social forms, just as the latter enters the room; and after some paragraphs of brilliant patter by James (enough to make us puzzled by the sequence): 'If that were true,' she said, 'I shouldn't tell you that I am very sorry to have kept you waiting.' Now Olive is represented throughout – it is the essence of her – as nervous, brusque, socially clumsy. She is moreover at that moment suffering from 'a fit of tragic shyness'. Yet James gives her this theatrically poised and elegant opening remark; because he wants a smooth transition at all costs.

On the whole, the characters in that novel are fully realised. In *What Maisie Knew* and *Washington Square*, the characters are mere outlines, identified by picturesque devices, on which the author then plays his variations and makes his comments, both of which are more vivid than the characters themselves. Maisie's father, for instance, consists almost entirely of a big beard and bright teeth; which are referred to with increasing ingenuity; his teeth becoming 'his shining fangs' by the end. Her mother is identified by her 'huge staring eyes' and 'painted like an idol'. James handles them both as if they were theatrical properties, tailor's dummies, wholly invariable and disposable. 'They made up together, for instance, some twelve foot three inches of stature, and nothing was more discussed than the apportionment of this quantity.'

All the kinds of technical brilliancy James displayed have a special relation to the theatre of his time, where Wilde also developed his sensibility; the well-made play having so much worldly sophistication and technical brilliance, so little of the kind of realism we associate with George Eliot. And of course James wanted passionately to write plays himself, and admits, in his prefaces, the influence of the theatre.

One consequence of this enthusiasm is an obviousness which is at odds with his air of subtlety. Again it is striking that this is to be found not only in the late work, after his venture in the theatre, but in something as early as *Washington Square*. Both Mrs Penniman and Morris Townsend are played for laughs. Mrs Penniman's intellectual pretentiousness is indicated by her speaking of seeing the ruins of the Pantheon in Europe; and this rather unsubtle joke is repeated at her expense more than once. Another time she says: 'I pay the penalty in my headaches, my famous headaches – a perfect circlet of pain! But I carry it as a queen carries a crown.' This can only be swallowed as a moment of broad farce. Morris is given some very stagy moments at the ends of chapters. ' "My dear good girl", he exclaimed, looking down at his prize. And then he looked up again, rather vaguely, with parted lips and lifted eyebrows.' The relations of these two with each other consist almost entirely of stagy gestures – Morris lights his cigar with Mrs Penniman's letter to him. Such writing contrasts grossly with James's air of avoiding the obvious, let alone the loud, of transforming always the crudities of experience into subtle art. Does he find experience *this* crude, one asks? Or does he think *these* gestures the elements of a subtle art language?

A more profound consequence is a theatricality in the persons and themes James treats, as distinct from the way he treats them. Not only do we see of his characters only what they show in the (stage-set) drawing-room; we instinctively feel them to be creatures of that setting, more important, more at ease, more themselves there than in the kitchen or the bedroom or anywhere without an audience. For instance, in *The Europeans*, Eugenia and Felix are people meant to be seen across footlights. They are always doing the same things – Felix laughing, sketching, throwing back his head, Eugenia frowning, pacing, fanning – and these are things aimed at an audience. One cannot imagine them without that; one cannot imagine them in a relationship where there is no third person to appreciate their performance, and to appreciate it in the mood of a theatre audience. The presence of that audience is essential to the poise of the book's manner; without it Eugenia's manner to her uncle ('You are a *beau vieillard*, dear uncle') and Felix's to Mr Brand, seem coarse, brutal, even grotesque.

Felix in love with Gertrude is unreal for that reason. ' "I am very much in love with Gertrude," he said, "she is very interesting and very different from what she seems. She has never had a chance. She is very brilliant. We will go to Europe and amuse ourselves." ' As for Eugenia's marriage, it is unimaginable. And what are her feelings towards (as distinct from *about*) Robert Acton? As James says, Eugenia's principal joy was exerting power, making an impression; to which we can add that she needed to have someone see her do it. As Isabel discovers about Madame Merle (essentially the same character) she exists only in her social relations. That is why the past of both women, their 'wickedness', is so unreal, melodramatic, discontinuous with the substance of the story. Both women are really actresses; James is portraying the fascination of great stage-stars; theatricality is at the source of their charm, their power, their sophistication, their corruptness, and their wickedness. At the height of his passion, Robert Acton, looking at Eugenia, thinks: 'By Jove, how *comme il faut* she is', and wishes he could see her carrying all before her at Newport; and this is a love-cry appropriate to its object. Felix, like Sir Claude in *What Maisie Knew* and Vanderbank in *The Awkward Age*, is a *jeune premier*; someone *acting* a handsome young man.

More indirectly, this concern for technical brilliance brings out (encourages or legitimises) an unsatisfactory handling of some aspects of life. James felt he could put them off-stage, and then they would not really matter. The most obvious example here is the experience of love and marriage. Especially in his late work, James offers us personal relationships dominated, wholly animated, by motives like intellectual curiosity and moral discrimination; in which the actual marriages and love affairs are entirely subordinate. In *The Awkward Age*, for instance (and there are more flagrant cases), Mitchie marries Aggie to do Nanda a favour. But even in *The Portrait of a Lady* the relationship between Isabel and Osmond is dangerously thin in sexual or affectionate emotion, dangerously strong in impersonal appraisal, and we are told that Mr Bantling marries Henrietta to 'find out'. Stories like 'Flickerbridge' and 'The Figure in the Carpet' are most disturbing in their intimations of a complete loss of perspective; and even 'The Beast in the Jungle', which in some sense discusses this problem, arouses the same dismay; for the narrator's posthumously understood relationship to his confidante was still not a large enough thing to support the weight it is given at the end of the story.

The same unreality marks the treatment of other aspects of experience. In 'Brooksmith' both the central character's suicide and his employer's. natural end obtrude from the substance of the story. They have not been successfully incorporated, or even invoked; James's tone cannot handle them. The themes of personal superiority and social gradation cross clumsily with the facts of death. 'What had become of it however when Mr Offord passed away like an inferior person – was relegated to eternal stillness after the manner of a butler above-stairs.' The same is true of 'The Patagonia' (both stories have some fine things in them); the suicide cannot be reconciled with the general manner, the narrator's gossipy, even giggling, tone with Mrs Nettlepoint. Death and disease have to lose some of their reality before James can handle them; they have to become modes of rational behaviour; people (for instance, Ralph Touchett) stay alive out of curiosity.

At his best, in *The Portrait of a Lady*, James does not fail in this gross way with the large themes, but, like the treatment of Isabel's love, that of Ralph's death is dangerously thin in first-hand experience, dangerously much a matter of literary conventions skilfully manœuvred. One inevitably suspects some evasion of personal experience; and James's description of his mother's death (compared with his fine evocation of Minnie Temple's love of life, for instance) is disturbingly conventional, literary, rhetorical. But however it was in life, in his writing James too often relied on the social evaluations of personal experience, and exempted himself from severe probings. This shows itself in intellectual matters too; again one may instance from his own life his religious opinions; and in *The Bostonians*, one cannot feel satisfied that either Ransome, or James, really knows, much less has answered, the feminist case.

It is difficult to believe that Olive would not have had something more plausible to offer than phrases like 'the brutal, blood-stained, ravening race'. This would not matter if there were not so much evidence that Ransome and James are quite as passionately and unreasonably roused as the feminists. This is expressed, betrayed, in the continual laughing condescension (for instance, the treatment of Miss Birdseye) as well as in the occasional direct anger.

'Her description of the convention put the scene before him vividly; he seemed to see the crowded, overheated hall, which he was sure was filled with carpet-baggers, to hear flushed women, with loosened bonnet-strings, forcing thin voices into ineffectual shrillness. It made him angry, and all the more angry, that he hadn't a reason, to think of the charming creature at his side being mixed up with such elements, pushed and elbowed by them, conjoined with them in emulation, in unsightly strainings and clappings and shoutings, in windy wordy iteration of inanities. Worst of all was the idea that she should have expressed such a congregation to itself so acceptably, have been acclaimed and applauded by hoarse throats, have been lifted up, to all the vulgar multitude, as the queen of the occasion.'

With so much emotion invested in the issue, the reader needs reassuring that the writer has taken it seriously in every sense. The charming creature at his side isn't quite good enough.

None of this means that James is not a brilliant writer, or that *The Bostonians* and *The Portrait of a Lady* are not brilliant novels. The nature of that brilliance is set forth in Dr Leavis's *The Great Tradition*, and my disagreement is in a sense only a rider to that. But they are not great novels. I am offering reasons why we cannot yield James that fullness of control, that power of suggestivity, which we yield to the great. He has not 'added something'; not something we can accept. Because he did not know enough about the crucial experience fiction deals with, and he was always on the verge of an irreverence before life.

He did not know enough about, for instance, Felix and Eugenia in *The Europeans*. He did not get clear the distinction between real sophistication and their claim to be sophisticated; or between real charm and their claim to be charming. He did not take account of a theatricality in them, which would in real life signify a clumsiness, a timidity, a provinciality. He did not know enough about Van and Nanda in *The Awkward Age*. We recognise the types he is talking about, but we cannot accept his diagnosis of them. Nanda does not know too much; she acts too much; she is too aggressive, too managing, too interfering, too moralistic. Because her father has played at being a character, her mother at being a child, and Nanda has taken on the moral responsibility of the whole family from too young. *This* is what frightens Van, who is (like Sir Claude in *What Maisie Knew*) a much more timid and light-weight young man than James admits. Van has looks, brains, manners, enough to be desirable; and he has not force enough to be anything more; he laughs and throws his head back, and lets other people fight over him.

Even more damaging is that incipient irreverence before life which crystallises itself fleetingly in those Oscar Wilde moments. This is perhaps most striking in *Washington Square*. Robert Garis (in an essay in *Audit*, 1960) has explained James's almost unique importance by his combination of 'the urbane knowledgeability which comedy encourages and exemplifies' with 'the "reverently eager expectation" of life's opportunities'. One can see that both these are most strikingly present in *Washington Square*. But the combination is unsuccessful (as Mr Garis admits it often is). The urbanity shrivels up the eager reverence. James's language about Catherine (to whom he is genuinely eager to do justice, and pay homage) as it were involuntarily makes fun of her, echoes her father's sarcasms.

‘ It simply appeared to him proper and reasonable that a well-bred young woman should not carry half her fortune on her back. Catherine's back was a broad one, and would have carried a good deal . . .

Her main superiority being that while the bundle of shawls sometimes got lost, or tumbled out of the carriage, Catherine was always at her post, and had a firm and ample seat . . . . ’

The slight vulgarity in physical matters here is another example of the co-operation of James's zeal for sophistication with his imperfect sense of the real.

Neither of these modes of failure are major in the best novels, but they are not wholly absent. James does not so transcend himself there that we can recognise a new artistic personality. In *The Portrait of a Lady* there is a discontinuity between the corruptness of nature of Osmond and Madame Merle, the quality the novel beautifully realises, and the novelette intrigue between them it alleges. One cannot be sure that James even recognised that discontinuity; if he did, he signally failed to solve the problem it presents. The book ends badly, too (quite apart from Caspar Goodwood's intrusion) and in a way which reflects back on the whole; the last section, with Isabel's discovery and Ralph's death, is swollen with self-pity and self-dramatisation. Isabel 'slowly got up; standing there, in her white cloak, which covered her to her feet, she might have represented the angel of disdain, first cousin to that of pity'. Later, when Goodwood asks her if he can pity her, she rests her eyes on him over her fan. 'Don't give your life to it; but give a thought to it every now and then.' And Ralph, who left money to various 'people who at various times had seemed to like him', says to her: ' "And remember this," he continued, "That if you have been hated, you have also been loved." ' This is not the quality of great literature. And when you have separated off the good parts you find that you have impaired the novel's claim to be about life as a whole; it deals superbly with certain areas of social-moral life, but the connexion it alleges between these and the rest of experience is doubtful.

In *The Bostonians* the tone is not well enough controlled to prevent our feeling at times that its sophistication is too much like an unregenerate and philistine worldliness. James says of the Tarrants' experiments with new 'ideas', 'the couple lived in an atmosphere of novelty, in which, occasionally, the accommodating wife encountered the fresh sensation of being in want of her dinner'. There is a brittleness in the imagination behind that sentence. One quite admits that the Tarrants' ideas are not to be taken seriously; but Mrs Tarrant's hunger is not part of the humour; except for someone who can imagine hunger only as a social mishap, a lapse in respectability. Later Olive goes to a party at the Tarrants' house, preoccupied with the idea that she will have to pay them to let her keep Verena.

' Some image of this transaction, as one of the possibilities of the future, outlined itself for Olive among the moral incisions of the evening. It seemed implied in the very place, the bald bareness of Tarrant's temporary lair, a wooden cottage, with a rough front yard, a little naked piazza, which seemed rather to expose than to protect, facing upon an unpaved road, in which the footway was overlaid with a strip of planks. These planks were embedded in ice or in liquid thaw, according to the momentary mood of the weather, and the advancing pedestrian traversed them in the attitude, and with a good deal of the suspense, of a rope-dancer. There was nothing in the house to speak of; nothing, to Olive's sense, but a smell of kerosene; though she had a consciousness of sitting down somewhere — the object creaked and rocked beneath her — and of the table at tea being covered with a cloth stamped in bright colours. ,

The lively distaste here, the accusations of vulgarity, attaches itself embarrassingly to the results of ignorance and poverty; more important, it is continuous with, undistinguished from, the accusation of moral failure. That lack of distinction is disturbing, and prevents full response.

This novel has also been very fortunate in its history. Its treatment of social problems, and above all its treatment of sexual morality in the largest sense, has been given, by the work of subsequent writers, a dignity which deceives us. Lionel Trilling* says: 'He has the courage of the collateral British line of romantic conservatives — he is akin to Yeats, Lawrence, and Eliot in that he experiences his cultural fears in the most personal way possible, translating them into sexual fear, the apprehension of the loss of manhood.' This, to my sense, is not true. 'The sentiment of sex' James referred to in the novel is for him a purely social thing, a code of manners. 'Loss of manhood' could be for him only a disturbance of decorum, a prevalence of ugly social challenges, and its apprehension only what is expressed in the passage on the female convention. James's ideal of womanhood was expressed in his lines on his mother.

⁶ It was a perfect mother's life — the life of a perfect wife. To bring her children into the world — to expend herself, for years, for their happiness and welfare — then, when they had reached a full maturity and were absorbed in the world and their own interests — to lay herself down in her ebbing strength and yield up her pure soul to the celestial power that had given her this divine commission. ,

*In his introduction to the Chiltern Library edition of the novel.

This is a purely Victorian ideal, with nothing of the sexual vitality we associate with Lawrence's or even Yeats's 'romantic conservatism'. We nowadays are almost inevitably deceived, with our ultra-sophisticated sense of sex, by James's quite phenomenal innocence in the matter. When he speaks of Olive Chancellor's 'sex', we inevitably think he means *some* comment on her sexuality. But in fact he merely refers to her social category. For instance, '. . . the emancipation of Olive Chancellor's sex (what sex was it, great heavens, he used profanely to ask himself) . . .' He could not have written that if his mind were turning itself – however discreetly – to the forces that make for sexual health or unhealth. We instinctively assume that though he could not be thinking of the clinical classifications of perversity, he was in his way aware of the reality beneath. But if he had been, that phrase would have been red-hot to him, and it clearly was not; it merely means she was not womanly. James seems to be playing with fire throughout the book; but for him there was no fire.

Above all, *The Bostonians* is short of greatness by the degree to which its tone fails in masculinity, by its own criteria.

'. . . it's a feminine, a nervous, chattering, canting age, an age of hollow phrases and false delicacy and exaggerated solicitudes and coddled sensibilities.'

With all its intelligence, the book contains examples of all those vices, and this failure makes its handling of its main theme insecure, unauthoritative.

Yet Dr Leavis says of the 'easy reference to Comte' at the beginning of *The Bostonians*, that the reader 'feels' James has the right to it. 'Not that we suppose him to have made a close study of Comte – or to have needed to.' That is, James and the book have imposed themselves on the reader as authoritative; we are ready to trust James, and dismiss Positivism as an inflection of his narrative voice. And Lionel Trilling says it is hard to understand the offence taken in Boston at the portrayal of Miss Birdseye (presumed to be drawn from Elizabeth Peabody), and says it is the tenderest and most endearing portrait imaginable. This again can only be because he has accepted and trusted James's point of view completely; for from her own point of view one cannot imagine a more condescending account of a career, refusing to discuss whether there was any sense or use in it, honouring her 'innocence', her 'simplicity', joking about her appearance. Both these remarks are the results of a surrender to James more complete than the novels seem to me to justify, and of the malign influence of that surrender. For both Leavis and Trilling, in assenting to James, are dismissing too easily the claims of social and political thought to be taken seriously on their own terms. The effect of such assents and such dismissals on the sensibility as a whole seems also demonstrated in Dr Leavis, where the case is particularly clear because of the equally obvious and seemingly opposite influence of D. H. Lawrence. The Jamesian heritage in Leavis's thought is summed up in the quotation at the beginning of this chapter: '. . . a nuance may engage a whole complex moral economy, and the perceptive response be the index of a major valuation or choice'. This habit of vision James certainly has 'added', for Leavis, whose whole controversial manner is based on the recognition of and response to such nuances; they are the source both of his obliquity and of his moral intensity. More importantly, his theory of culture as a whole is based on the belief that there is no moral economy too complex to be engaged by a nuance; no kind of intellectual activity

which is not in fact adequately represented in sophisticated language, and consequently subject to the final
arbitration of the literary critic.

James teaches one to include moral considerations
in aesthetic judgements, but then makes the latter
obliquely autonomous – with power not only over novels
but over what they deal with, including Positivism,
feminism, abolition, the whole of life. This is why
James has been so seductive, and why so many people
have wanted to call him great. He makes it seem that
aesthetic sensibility, suitably enlarged, will guide you
through every moral and intellectual tangle. But neither
his novels themselves nor the vision of life they embody
justify us in agreeing with him.

Faulkner:

the triumph of rhetoric

'... a long corridor of grey halflight where all stable things had become shadowy paradoxical all I had done shadows all I had felt suffered taking visible form antic and perverse mocking without relevance inherent themselves with the denial of the significance they should have affirmed. '

All that is wrong with the writer's work is summed up in this passage from *The Sound and the Fury*. Both by the statement, which describes metaphorically what Faulkner's rhetoric in fact does to its subject-matter; and by the style, which is a fair example of *how* he does it – the monotone, the endlessness, the insensitive emphasis, the flatulent and often fulsome vocabulary, the flashy contraventions of grammar and punctuation and typography. The style, as usual, so dominates the statement that our major evidence for the latter's authority (its qualities of intelligence, or passion, or realism) must be the quality of the 'style-in-itself'; and the latter's inert literariness (for instance, 'antic'), plus its chic experimentalism, tells us not to respond.

Faulkner had of course remarkable literary gifts; in the vein of sardonic humour best represented by Jason Compson, and in grotesque anecdotes like those of *As I Lay Dying*, he commands our liveliest attention; and the craftsmanship of his mimicry, his scene-building, all the techniques of his descriptive realism, and his fragmented narration, could be superb. What ruins those gifts is their assimilation into an elaborate and ambitious rhetoric which ruthlessly *imposes* itself on the subject-matter; on persons, events, motives, moods, themes; which gets between that subject-matter and the writer so that all the meaning is aborted. The events don't mean anything; one doesn't know how to respond to them. They are all immensely 'significant', but that is another matter; the emotion they arouse, or through which they are seen, is usually attributed to a character in the novel, not the author; and it is never so embodied in the rendering of the event, so co-operative with intelligent observation and reflection, that the reader can share it – can feel that same response growing in him. Thus there is no meaning; using 'meaning' here to describe an image's power to evoke a *precise* affective response, which involves both understanding and evaluation, as well as feeling. In Faulkner's novels, the reader knows that a lot of emotion is being demanded from him – the event is significant; but just what, and just why, he does not know – it is not meaningful.

Such emotion is external to the reader; external to the event, too, arbitrarily attached to it, since we have never been convinced that the event would *necessarily* call forth that response; and external to the writer himself, since the verbal rhetoric in which it is expressed is too loud, too consciously exaggerated, for us to trust it as the writer's sincere utterance. Indeed, the ruthless-ness, the irrelevance, with which this rhetoric is applied becomes one of its structural features; it adds another dimension of alienation – from the language itself. There is a distance, a space, between Faulkner and his characters, his events, even his sentences; so that we can never say, 'See, here, this is how Faulkner's mind works'. We must always say, 'This is how Faulkner's literary method works'. In D. H. Lawrence, a very different writer, we are always in touch with the writer's mind at its most sincere; and we are frequently given passages of direct experience; and the rhetoric, the method, is kept to a minimum. In Henry James, an author much more like Faulkner, there is little direct rendering of experience, but we are aware of an active intelligence at work in the prose, and though there is a formidable rhetoric, dangerously independent of its subject-matter, that rhetoric works with an elegance and brilliance which command much more of our response than Faulkner's.

The putative subject-matter in Faulkner is subjected to a formidable rhetorical machine; it is as it were fractionated by it; so that one no longer finds there the normal interplay between a critical intelligence and its passionate experience. The events and persons in Faulkner's novels seem to have been imagined, the moods felt, the ideas thought, mainly in order to supply this overweening literary method. We find no substantial, complex experience, no sharp, active intelligence, no interaction between the two, no total shape, no meaning. What we do find is a rhetoric gone crazy with unlimited power, and betraying itself again and again in demonstrable absurdities, infelicities, and errors.

For instance, language is used to create effects of significant eloquence which can often be *demonstrated* to be not meaningful (using meaning now in its simpler semantic sense). The reader is taught to register only the loudest meanings of a word, and to respond with only half his mind; and the half that is put out of commission is that closest to common sense. When we are told that T.P. wore 'cheap bright *intransigent* clothes', or that Jason divided up the '*vast* oncesplendid' rooms of the Compson house, we instinctively read the second as 'big', and the first we scarcely read at all. We recognise it as 'clever', a touch of colour on the surface of *The Sound and the Fury*, but no more deeply related to the book's meaning than a dozen alternative Tennessee Williams phrases. (I shall take all my examples from the works of Faulkner's 'great period'; from *The Sound and the Fury, As I Lay Dying*, and *Light in August*.) This is because we have been numbed, drunken, drowned, in a deluge of the largest language, which we later discovered was all to be repeated again in different contexts, and was quite vague and loose in its first (in any particular) use. We have learned that language is being used for large general effects, half the properties of the individual words and constructions being sacrificed to that end. We have seen meaning drain out of language.

One of the signs of this is simple tautology; 'identical and uniform', 'vocal and vociferant', 'domestic, uxorious, connubial', 'patented, sealed, and countersigned', 'not the refraining but the restraint'. Perhaps this is not simple tautology, since Faulkner implies that the distinctions are meaningful; but the text makes no use of those meanings, and the effect of the distinctions is finally just to repeat, to emphasise, to be sonorous, to relax the reader's attention. It is simple, however, by comparison with tautologies like 'the myriad coruscations of immolation and abnegation and time', or those of the Nobel Prize Address. These are tautologies only because the effect of the collocation of the words is to bring out in each what it has in common with the others, at the cost of every distinction, grammatical as well as semantic.

Another symptom of this loss of meaning is the mystification of 'I never even suspicioned then that what I didn't know was not the worst of it', or 'but above them all set not his wife's honor but the principle that honor must be defended whether it was or not because defended it was whether or not'; where the effort to sort out the syntax is not rewarded by any significant clarification or subtilisation of the meaning, and consequently the reader learns not to bother; the words and their meanings are merely a form of embroidery or ornament.

Another symptom (let us take these three as representing many more) is the long simile, sometimes elaborate, often violent, always violently at odds with the thing described. When the town ceases to persecute Hightower, it was

'As though, Byron thought, the entire affair had been a lot of people performing a play and that now at last they had all played out the parts which had been allotted to them and now they could live quietly with one another.   '

The normal sense of the event is violently inverted, with the effect of making it seem less real, and therefore in this case *less* dangerous. These similes always remove the thing described from the grasp of normal understanding, and thus frustrate any attempt at intelligent judgement. This effect is usually masked by the psychological appropriateness of the simile to the character who employs it, who is usually in a state of strained exhaustion. But when, as in this case, there is no such appropriateness, it becomes clear that the real function of the phrasing is to impose significance (and evade meaning) in the same way the tautologies do. It just gives the event it describes the Faulknerian flavour. Both the account of the town's persecution, and the picture of unwilling actors, lose their distinctness and their factuality, in exchange for the glamour of illustrating 'the author's vision of life'.

Moreover these similes are often so mechanical that you feel the writer has quite lost contact with his image; that for him, as for the reader, this simile is only another example of his general technique; so that meaning drains out of the language in a different sense. Thus Hightower finds reading Tennyson is 'like listening in a cathedral to a eunuch chanting in a language which he does not even need to not understand'. The reader does not bother to work out the inversions at the end; he does not respond to the total scene; he registers only the words 'eunuch' and 'chanting'. And sometimes the author's control is so loose that the simile becomes – if the reader is not too hypnotised to realise it – outrageous. Thus Quentin

‘ loved not his sister's body but some concept of Compson honor precariously and (he knew well) only temporarily supported by the minute fragile membrane of her maidenhead as a miniature replica of the whole vast globy earth may be poised on the nose of a trained seal.   ’

Here all the parallels – Caddy and a trained seal, the tip of its lifted nose and her maidenhead, a ball balancing there and the family honor, and the sudden intrusion of 'the whole vast globy earth' – are as preposterous as any that could be devised. All that can be said for the simile is that it diverts attention from the highly implausible 'concept of honor' Quentin is alleged to believe in. But perhaps the most interesting point is that people learn to read Faulkner – intelligent readers do – so faithfully, in such obedience to the signals he sends out, that they read this with no disturbance to their sense of his genius.

This love of certain effects of language, like the other elements of his rhetoric, is allowed to run amok; it tramples down all sorts of propriety of characterisation, for instance. The thoughts of Darl Bundren, who is totally uneducated, are presented in terms like re-accruent and non-inferant; 'mileboards becoming more starkly re-accruent' and 'non-inferant of progress'. It tramples down all propriety of narration when simple actions are to be described. When Joe Christmas, at five years old, steals somebody's toothpaste to eat, Faulkner intones: 'On that first day when he discovered the toothpaste in her room he had gone directly there, who had never heard of toothpaste either, as if he already knew that she would possess something of that nature and he would find it.' When the same character resents a woman's sewing the buttons on after washing his clothes,

‘ he set himself deliberately to learn and remember which buttons were missing and had been restored. With his pocket knife and with the cold and bloodless deliberation of a surgeon he would cut off the buttons which she had just replaced.　　　　　　’

The tautology, 'learn and remember', the simile 'with the cold and bloodless deliberation of a surgeon', the doomed automatism, 'as if he already knew', the sinister heroism of will-power, 'deliberately'; all are unrolled here – where they couldn't be more inappropriate – just as solemnly as elsewhere; because they are the regular functions of Faulkner's unstoppable machine.

This machine, this rhetoric, is disengageable from its subject-matter. You could apply it to absolutely anything. You can construct it in mid-air, out of relation to a subject. You take the vocabulary, 'frozen . . . furious . . . unbelieving . . . unseeing . . . doomed . . . damned . . .'; you build long sentences with complicated negatives, 'what he did not even know was not . . .' and 'not because . . . and not because . . .'; you use images of frozen motion, 'found himself running before he even knew he . . . ' and 'was still crying it when . . .' you add long similes of automatism, 'It was as though . . .'; and you sprinkle the sentences with *even*, and *either*, and *himself*.

Faulkner himself offers us this rhetoric *in vacuo*; he applies it so regularly and inappropriately that we are made conscious of it as a thing in itself, and this consciousness becomes another way of alienating the author from his language, of dissipating meaning. It declares him not responsible, not answerable to the reader, either for fully rendering the thing described, or for the feelings about it he is expressing; he has arbitrarily invented the scene, and now arbitrarily imposes a significance on it. This significance, these feelings, cannot be taken simply as the author's because they are attributed to a character. This constitutes the original invitation to 'interpret', so enthusiastically taken up by Faulkner critics; this much can be found in many novelists; but the loud, mechanical, self-sustaining character of Faulkner's rhetoric, the gap between it and the writer, makes *his* invitation virtually limitless. There are no strings attached. It is like playing tennis with the net down. Because there are no meanings already there to trip you up – no meanings inherent in both the events and the language, and the whole shape of the book. Thus evasion of responsibility by the novelist has invited invasion by the critics; it is precisely what is wrong with Faulkner which has aroused so much interpretative enthusiasm; bad writing in him has produced bad writing in them.

The use of language is only part of the total rhetoric, however; certain structural devices are equally directed to the evasion of meaning, and are equally crude and exaggerated in application. The indirect narration, for instance, so typical of Faulkner, is a way to not tell us what *he* thinks of a character or event. It is always

Quentin's or Caddy's ·picture of Herbert Head we get. It is also a way to not expose to our judgement his understanding of individual psychology, or social mechanics, or anything else. We never see whether Faulkner himself has any more understanding of the type than this purely conventional outline.

This device is applied as mechanically as the tricks of language. We find it in contexts of every degree of appropriateness, and in some where it is demonstrably inappropriate. In *Light in August*, for instance, quite unliterary people like Byron Bunch and Mrs Hines recount episodes from their own past, but using all the panoply of Faulknerian rhetoric. Byron even imagines episodes at which he was not present, and invents motives and feelings for people he has never seen; for instance, in the case of the countryman who discovered the fire at Miss Burden's; Faulkner is making practically no pretence that this is really Byron's mind at work.

But quite apart from their inappropriateness, these devices cost Faulkner heavily, in the fullness of response he can win from his readers. Richard Chase says that 'it is hard to see that', in *As I Lay Dying*,

> ‘ . . . much has been gained by Faulkner's elaborate procedure. On the other hand, not much has been lost, and once the reader is prepared to accept or ignore the few surrealistic excesses of image and language, there is little to disconcert him and much to excite his admiration. ’

But something more has been lost, which very much affects our admiration. The reader has been denied the chance to find out if Faulkner knows how someone like Addie Bundren behaves, how the sophisticated and primitive blend in her speech, what her relations are with, say, Darl. All this 'understanding' of the woman, which would, if it convinced us, open our responses to every appeal Faulkner has to make *about* her, is, by this indirect narration and 'multiple point of view', obviated, obscured, made to disappear by sleight of hand.

It is no surprise that when the narrative is direct, and the author is speaking for once in his own voice, as for instance in the flashback over Joe Christmas's early life, another narrative feature becomes prominent. We are told that a character 'perhaps' thought this, or 'perhaps' felt that emotion; 'perhaps' he was doing it for this or that ideal, or for the sake of this or that person; 'perhaps' he did not know why he had to do this, he only knew he must. It is in this uncertainty, this multi-valency, about his characters and events, that Faulkner reminds us most of Hawthorne and the whole line of American. romance.

It might seem that the novels' passages of stark realism constitute an exception to the rule about them so far developed; both because the realistic mode submits the characters and events it describes to the reader's common-sense critical scrutiny, and because it gives them some three-dimensional independent reality, and thus saves them from complete dependence on their inventor's arbitrary purposes. But realism in Faulkner is a superficial and intermittent technique. He gives his characters, for example, dialect words and country images even when he is making them do things in every profound sense at variance with their social and psychological types. When the author has a point to make, or even just a metaphor to use, he rides rough-shod over personal and social psychology. The large-scale examples of this are the dialogues between Bunch and Hightower, but it can be illustrated by this exchange (also from *Light in August*):

 ' Mooney said: "Well, Simms is safe from hiring anything at all when he put that fellow on. He never even hired a whole pair of pants."

"That's so", Byron said. "He puts me in mind of one of these cars running along the street with a radio in it. You can't make out what it is saying and the car ain't going anywhere in particular and when you look at it close you see that there ain't even anybody in it."

"Yes", Mooney said. "He puts me in mind of a horse. Not a mean horse. Just a worthless horse. Looks fine in the pasture, but it's always down in the spring bottom when anybody comes to the gate with a bridle. Runs fast, all right, but it's always got a sore hoof when hitching-up time comes."

"But I reckon maybe the mares like him", Byron said.

"Sho", Mooney said. "I don't reckon he'd do even a mare any permanent harm." ⁹

This is an exercise in folk metaphor, not a conversation. In fact, Faulkner's realism has the same effect as devices like indirect narration; because it appears and disappears so arbitrarily that the reader is reduced even more to dependence on short-term signs – he can never learn the rules of autonomous response, of critical co-operation with the author. It is also, of course, a way of deflecting criticism, to be able to attribute any crudity of feeling to the character, any profundity to the author.

A typical form of realism in Faulkner is the strained and unnatural narration of every detail of a period of waiting before some undisclosed violent action. For instance, Joe Christmas's day before killing Miss Burden, and Quentin Compson's day before committing suicide. There is some general appeal to our sense of reality (the reality of mental disturbance), but most of the time the reader is obliged to follow the writer's lead in total bewilderment. The method has its successes, as in the episode of the Italian girl who attaches herself to Quentin Compson; it has its demonstrable failures, as in the pomposities of 'Memory believes before knowing remembers'; but most of the time the reader moves in limbo, unable to say yes or no to what is offered him, conscious only that he has still been given no reason to *trust* the author's appeals to respond to these images.

It is in *Light in August* that this narrative rhetoric is applied most crudely and clumsily. It distorts and ruins both extraordinary events like McEachern beating Joe for not learning his catechism, and comparatively ordinary ones like the Hines's waiting for the train to Jefferson. The determination to make the event significant is so loud, its manner so crudely external to the subject, its detail so ill-considered and tasteless, that the reader is alienated from both book and author.

When we come to the characterisation we find that the psychological types and the lives Faulkner chooses to write about have the same qualities of violence or monotony or hollow grandeur as his vocabulary and his narrative methods; and therefore equally elude our discriminative scrutiny. His people are abnormal and alienated types, insane, drunken, or criminal, desperate, defeated, or immemorially serene. We can often recognise their relationship to the stock types of conventional melodrama. We can never recognise their relationship to ourselves; for these people live their whole lives in psychological states which we undergo very rarely and which we regard even at the time as unnatural; states of automatism in which they are not responsible for what they are doing, and watch themselves and their actions from outside. These states, and hence these characters, baffle our intelligence; apart from a crude estimate of their case-book orthodoxy, our critical scrutiny can get no grip on them; they are the antithesis and reverse of the mental condition we are in as we read the novel. All we have to guide our response is the author's method, which is often demonstrably crude.

For instance, the characters of *The Sound and the*

Fury are almost frankly derived from either stage melo-drama or light fiction. This is sometimes given away by the stock phrase which was their inspiration (though Faulkner usually avoids or conceals this phrase), some-times by their names. Thus the librarian is named Melissa Meek, and is also called 'a mouse-coloured, mouse-sized spinster'; but Herbert Head, Caddy's vulgar fiancé, is never called a cad, though he is fitted out with a cigar, a 'little widow over in town', and he cheats at cards, cheats at exams, and tries to bribe Quentin. But when Quentin says, 'I don't know but one way to consider cheating. I don't think I'm likely to learn different at Harvard', we know where we have met Herbert before; he is the Black Sheep of St Dominic's, the lout in loud checks who sneaked away from games to smoke and back horses. Mr and Mrs Compson fit equally neatly into stock phrases. She is 'weak and cold'; he is 'a scholar and a gentleman' but 'cynical and self-indulgent'; we have often met him at some outpost of the Empire, whither an early indiscre-tion had exiled him at the start of a brilliant career, in the novels of P. C. Wren or E. Phillips Oppenheim. Caddy, beautiful and damned, cold, serene, and damned (these phrases are actually used about her) is the beauti-ful, wilful, high-spirited girl who takes the wrong turn-ing, and ends up a cold, proud, wealthy woman of fashion. She occurs in a hundred Victorian novels; Lady Dedlock is an example. She has been fitted out with a modern-style nymphomania; but this is completely external, completely unrelated to anything else in her. Quentin is the sensitive young man of twentieth-cen-tury fiction; he takes his origin (Stephen Dedalus, pre-sumably) from a more respectable class of literature, and hence is handled more gingerly. Jason too owes a good deal to conventional outlines, like the wicked bailiff, the landlord who forecloses the mortgage, the usurping uncle, and, when Faulkner describes his looks, 'a bar-tender in caricature'. But Jason is a genuine creation; in him we see how the method should work; Faulkner shows us the wicked bailiff-type in modern life and from inside. But when, as with the rest of the characters, the original material remains untransformed, remains clearly recognisable in (frequently) all its cheapness, no critical reader can begin to respond.

Even when the literary model is not obvious, the figures have the same flamboyance of gesture, the same exaggeration of outline. When Quentin tries to hit Dalton Ames, Caddy's lover, the latter 'held both my wrists in the same hand, his other hand flicked to his armpit under his coat' to get out a pistol; he drops a piece of bark into the stream below them, waits till it has floated out of shot, and 'afterwards the pistol came up he didn't aim at all the bark disappeared then pieces of it floated up spreading he hit two more of them pieces of bark no bigger than silver dollars'; Ames reloads the pistol ('he blew into the barrel a thin wisp of smoke dissolved he reloaded the three chambers, shut the cylinder he handed it to me butt first') and gives it to Quentin so that the latter can shoot him; then Quentin again tries to hit him and faints. Male swagger is given the kind of crude glamorisation we associate with Hollywood. But the point is not only the crudity of execution in a particular case; it is also the lack of appeal in all cases to our intelligence; neither Quentin's nor the reader's intelligence can get any grip on Dalton Ames, to understand or judge him. Nor is there any appeal in him to our experience – nothing is heard or seen which strikes us as recognisably true. We can neither understand nor recognise him. We can only accept him as a device of Faulkner's rhetoric.

Similar things can be found in the other books. For instance, everything about Lucas Burch in *Light in*

August is circumscribed by the phrase 'weakly handsome'; everything about McEachern by 'coldly righteous' and 'bigoted and ruthless'; about Miss Burden by 'New England spinster'. But more often the characters are composites; they combine features representing several of Faulkner's themes. Hightower and Joe Christmas are typical Faulkner characters of this kind. The unfrocked priest, the obsession with time, the Southern heritage; and the criminal, the rootless man, the race problem. In no case are they built or handled so as to convince us that they are real, or so as to show us anything about the way human nature works. They are built and handled to serve the purposes of Faulkner's rhetoric exclusively; to be loudly evocative, luridly significant, in sixteen ways, without committing the writer fully to develop any one of them. They are just vivid outlines and blank surfaces, people seen from angles and in attitudes where their normal complexity is simplified down to a caricature; those who are categorisably 'cads' or 'spinsters' are only a special case of this. We are not allowed, therefore, to understand or judge them as human beings. We are not allowed to use our intelligence on them or on their creator.

This is not to be explained away as due to the social type of Faulkner's characters, or to his describing them 'from outside', or to his writing 'romance-novel' fiction as distinct from, say, George Eliot realism. D. H. Lawrence's characters also exist largely in non-rational states, but those states are not anti-intelligent. We can compare, for instance, Pussum in *Women in Love* with the waitress in *Light in August*, a very similar character, and used to very similar effect:

'She was not only not tall, she was slight, almost childlike. But the adult look saw that the smallness was not due to any natural slenderness but to some inner corruption of the spirit itself; a slenderness which had never been young, in not one of whose curves anything youthful had ever lived or lingered.   '

Lawrence's character is described in more scattered sentences:

'She was small and delicately made with warm colouring and large dark hostile eyes. There was a delicacy, almost a beauty in all her form, and at the same time a certain attractive grossness of spirit, that made a little spark leap instantly alight in Gerald's eyes. . . . She was so profane, almost slave-like, watching him, absorbed by him. . . . She had been wearing a loose dressing gown of purple satin, tied around her waist. She looked so small and childish and vulnerable, almost pitiful.   '

We see immediately the crude and excessive emphasis in the Faulkner. We see the looseness of language – 'lived or lingered'. We see how Lawrence lets us see his girl in different ways even while keeping to as sharply single a point about her as Faulkner. Above all we see that we ourselves are involved with Lawrence's girl; she is made attractive and interesting to our minds even in that critical poise and complexity they have assumed to read the novel. Our *intelligence* is involved. This is what Faulkner never does, and that is why there is no fully personal experience in his novels. You can see the same kind of difference between Addie Bundren in *As I Lay Dying* and Mrs Morel in *Sons and Lovers*; and between Lucas Burch in *Light in August* and Rico Carrington in *St Mawr*.

Among the events and objects of the novels some are simply and conventionally melodramatic in the way the Compsons are as characters. For instance, the relic of Caddy that is preserved to quieten Benjy when he gets upset is a white satin slipper, 'yellow now, and cracked, and soiled'. And in *As I Lay Dying* Addie's illegitimate child is by the evangelical minister; and the latter's name is Whitfield; and the bastard, who is called Jewel, is the wildest and harshest of her children. And at the end of a long sequence of sordid description and violent action in *Light in August*, Mrs Hines delivers this speech:

'Eupheus. You listen to me. You got to listen to me. I ain't worried you before. In thirty years I ain't worried you. But now I am going to. I am going to know and you got to tell me. What did you do with Milly's baby?'

Which takes us right back to the first act curtain of something like *Lady Audley's Secret*.

Great use is also made of histories, extended anecdotes, family or personal, that enshrine some act of less conventional but still semi-legendary violence or horror; Joe Christmas's story, the Burdens' family history, the Compsons', and so on. These defy assimilation as personal experience; they categorically cannot be understood as the result of normal motivation; and yet they are cardinal features of Faulkner's characters' experience. This experience must then be a helpless brooding *around* the story – Hightower may be taken as the type-case – and a devaluation, a diminishment, of their own day-by-day life in contrast. What the stories mean to the author seems to be much the same. He is obsessed with them, broods over them, and rehearses them in the novel so that they may produce the same effect on the reader.

The events that take place in the present tend to be equally violent and equally unassimilable. When McEachern discovers Joe Christmas slipping out at night, he follows him on horseback,

'. . . at that slow and ponderous gallop, the two of them, man and beast, leaning a little stiffly forward as though in some juggernautish simulation of terrific speed though the actual speed itself was absent, as if in that cold and implacable and undeviating conviction of both omnipotence and clairvoyance of which they both partook destination and speed were not necessary. ,

(This must surely be the only cart-horse in literature with a cold and implacable and undeviating conviction of its omnipotence and clairvoyance.) He enters the dance-hall and hits Joe 'in the furious and dreamlike exaltation of a martyr'; Joe kills him (presumably), and steals his foster-mother's savings, and goes to marry his prostitute, all in the same state. Intelligence is explicitly excluded from such behaviour, and therefore, like the characters, these events elude our critical scrutiny – and therefore never win access to those depths of response in us which only our satisfied scrutiny will unlock.

Moreover, like every other feature of this rhetoric, this presentation of events becomes so exaggerated that the events' reality is openly sacrificed. In *Light in August*, when the man who discovered the Burden fire is mentioned a second time, there is a long parenthesis,

‘(he had not yet got to town; his wagon had not progressed one inch since he descended from it two hours ago, and he now moved among the people, wildhaired, gesticulant, with on his face a dulled, spent, glaring expression and his voice hoarsed almost to a whisper) ,

No reader believes there really was such a man; he is plainly conjured up to serve as a lay-figure for one more exercise in 'Faulknerism'. And this exaggeration becomes so crude that its statements, again and again, are literary howlers to the most sympathetically unprejudging reader. In *The Sound and the Fury* we are told that Quentin wanted to copulate with Caddy in order to make sure they would both go to hell, 'where he could guard her forever and keep her forevermore intact amid the eternal fires'; and that he was afraid to try to persuade her to do so because 'i was afraid to i was afraid she might'. We are told that Caddy loved Quentin 'because of the fact that he himself was incapable of love'; and that she, since he loved death better than her, would 'and perhaps in the calculation and deliberation of her marriage did' drive him to suicide. We are told that Jason thought of himself 'his file of soldiers in the rear, dragging Omnipotence down from His throne, if necessary; of the embattled legions of both hell and heaven through which he tore his way and put his hands at last on his fleeing niece'; and that 'Of his niece he did not think at all, nor the arbitrary valuation of the money. Neither of them had had entity or individuality for him for ten years; together they merely symbolised the job in the bank of which he had been deprived before he had ever got it.'

In all these cases, in different ways, we feel that Faulkner does not know what he is saying – does not know the reality he is talking about. The events and persons have lost reality for him, in the excitement of making a rhetorical point. We do not believe that Quentin wanted to copulate with Caddy – or that she might have agreed to; we do not believe that she deliberately drove him to suicide – or that she loved him for his impotence; we do not believe that Jason was uninterested in the money he lost or his niece. Fictional truth is flexible and many-faceted, but surely *these* statements can be declared flatly untrue, on the evidence of the characters' behaviour? And if God, and eternal punishment, and copulation, and love, were such flimsy fancies to these people as the sentences declare, then they were scarcely human beings at all; but in fact, of course, it is Faulkner to whom these ideas, these enormous facts, are so flimsy and fanciful; in the machine of his rhetoric they are reduced to units as smooth and glib (and nonsensical) as the word 'arbitrary' in the phrase 'arbitrary valuation of the money'.

Sometimes, so loose is Faulkner's grasρ of his facts, we find a version of them in one part of a book which is hard to reconcile with the version given later on. Thus Hightower's grandfather is at one time said to have been shot 'from a galloping horse', at another 'in a hen-house'. But this is merely a picturesque case of this looseness, the real evil of which is the reduction of imaginative events to the status of rhetorical units.

Faulkner's values are somewhat obscured by his rhetoric, so powerfully directed to the dissipation of all meaning. There are a great many value-words thrown around which reduce themselves, on examination, to very little. He has the habit, moreover, of throwing out hints of the most grandiose kind. Richard Chase says,

' It seems hard to be much impressed with the fact that Faulkner calls one of his characters "Joe Christmas", and that he is 33 years old, has his feet votively bathed, and is in a manner crucified. '

But though one cannot be impressed, one can be irritated; for the hints are there, to be responded to, one way or the other; Faulkner has put that idea into the reader's mind, useless and silly though it is. In *As I Lay Dying* Addie Bundren says that Jewel 'is my cross and will be my salvation. He will save me from the water and from the fire. Even though I have laid down my life, he will save me.' And after her death, in various unexpected and accidental ways, he does so; the main events of the book add up to the story of his doing it. What then does this prophecy mean to the reader? What version of religious feeling is it meant to introduce into our responses? How does it link up with the other material in the book? Not at all. Like the Christ-figure hints of *Light in August*, it has merely been added. Faulkner himself is the first, and by no means the best, of that army of sophomore symbol-hunters who buzz round his novels. Despite his Mississippi-farmer persona, it is no accident that Faulkner has attracted so much arty exegesis. Richard Chase, talking again about *As I Lay Dying*, apologises for

‘ . . . such attempts at "art" as making one of the characters repeat "My mother is a fish". Faulkner has always had a weakness for this kind of sophistication, with its suggestion of recondite symbolism. ’

But Mr Chase does not admit how much of the work this weakness infects, nor how much uncertainty it betrays in the book's basic aim.

Values are nevertheless clearly discernible in Faulkner's work. Their characteristic is that only the very simplest, in fact the consciously crude, are unambiguous. Everything more ambitious, like religious feeling, or family pride, or moral enthusiasm, or even beauty, brains, sensitiveness, are shown to end in disaster; and in no accidental way; good things are *bound* to fail. This preoccupation with failure makes a bridge between the romantic and the naturalistic modes in his imagination, just as it does in that of Graham Greene; Mr Compson's drinking is both the romantic gesture of a noble nature in ruin, and, seen through Jason's eyes, a study in seedy alcoholism. Thus these ambitious values are quite ambiguous. Fine qualities are a good thing but also a bad thing at the same time; a noble nature includes the principle of its own quite sordid self-destruction. Truths like this occur to all the intelligent and honest characters as they reflect. All moral and intellectual sophistication is an advance towards hopelessness – as we see in Mr Compson and the Reverend Hightower. This hopelessness, this complete scepticism, is shared moreover by the effectively good and responsible characters, like Peabody in *As I Lay*

Dying and the Sheriff in *Light in August*. Peabody has discovered death to be a mental, not a physical event, occurring in the minds of the spectators, not the patient; and Cash Bundren sees that the insanity of an act is constituted by the way other people happen to be looking at it when it occurs. These are the men Faulkner admires, and the values they do affirm are deflationary and reductive, consciously simple and traditional. Thus Mr Compson says that his children have learned cleanliness and honesty, 'which was all that anybody could hope to be taught'. And the author himself makes cheating at cards the token of Herbert Head's essential wrongness. His attitude to women, it has been pointed out, Faulkner shares with folk mythology; and his attitude to negroes is equally conventional. Their massive virtues, like their weaknesses, have a simpler, broader, more childlike cast than white people's; they don't know the agonies of moral choice. We have seen the glamour given to crude male assertiveness in the scene with Dalton Ames; and the contempt for its opposite in the comments on Lucas Burch.

It is thus values of a very simple, horsy kind we find in Faulkner; but they are also highly sophisticated, by their awareness of their own simplicity. This does not make them ambiguous and self-destructive, like the more romantic values; on the contrary, it makes them highly truculent and aggressive. For they bring with them also a corrosive scepticism about every other attitude to life. Faulkner's picture of life is suffused by his preoccupation with failure – the experience of betrayal, by oneself or the world, is the beginning of consciousness for most of his characters – and that feeling has all the misery of a personal disappointment made general. When we emerge into the light of day, in the fourth section of *The Sound and the Fury*, when we see the characters and places from Faulkner's point of view at last, it is a bleak and chill light:

> ' ... a moving wall of grey light out of the northwest which, instead of dissolving into moisture, seemed to disintegrate into minute and venomous particles, like dust that, when Dilsey opened the door of her cabin, and emerged, needled laterally into her flesh. '

This is an effective moment in the book, and part of its effectiveness is due to our feeling that we are at last seeing the Compson house and its occupants for ourselves, as they really are; it is therefore significant that the quality emphasised in nature is a kind of spitefulness.

Let us take two final examples of the Faulknerian procedure. Jason is described as 'The first sane Compson since before Culloden and (a childless bachelor) hence the last. Logical rational contained and even a philosopher in the old stoic tradition.' Now it needs no proof that Jason is not particularly sane; he is scarcely even rational; and it is not worth wondering what Faulkner thought the old stoic tradition was. The point of the remark is to imply that Quentin, Caddy, and Mr Compson are all *in*sane. The word is used too loosely to be sharply meaningful, but we gather that it is more 'normal', it is 'better', to behave like Jason than like the other three. The whole point of the book is that these three are infinitely more glamorous, noble, and beautiful, but when Faulkner makes this bitter, sulky, almost spiteful, innuendo, we realise that he is in fact strongly attracted to the opposite point of view. Not that Jason is sane, but that the noble, beautiful, and sensitive, are in a sense insane. They should have more *sense* than to be noble.

Later we read,

> ' ... his father, now completing the third of his three avatars – the

one as son of a brilliant and gallant statesman, the second as battle-leader of brave and gallant men, the third as a sort of privileged Daniel Boone–Robinson Crusoe, who had not returned to juvenility because actually he had never left it.

Here we have the actual assertion of the consciously romantic values, 'brilliant and gallant, brave and gallant', followed immediately by their devaluation, 'who had not returned to juvenility, because actually he had never left it'. These are the 'visible forms' of my opening quotation, 'inherent themselves with the denial of the significance they should have affirmed'. This is the typical Faulknerian procedure; to betray the romantic values he loves and offer only their antitheses in exchange.

What then does Faulkner believe in? Only in the consciously ambiguous or the aggressively inadequate; which is a form of unbelief. This is what makes the Appendix to *The Sound and the Fury*, and so much else of Faulkner's, almost classically bad writing. This enormous rhetoric is inspired by something that denies itself, something that only half exists; it is directed at problems declared to be insoluble, on behalf of values declared to be invalid, investigating truths declared to be unknowable. This mood of unbelief is the inspiration of the rhetoric. That is why the writer so arbitrarily *invents*; people who do not exist, events that never happened, emotions no one ever felt. That is why he avoids scenes of normal satisfaction and successful moral effort, and why the most vivid moods of Faulknerian people and Faulknerian nature are a sardonic vulgarity and a vicious spitefulness. He constructs an enormous universe to demonstrate the way things are *not*. The smell of death is over it all; not the corruption of the once living so much as the 'grey halflight' of Limbo, the meaningless mimicry of living forms.

It is impossible to make a statement about Faulkner that would answer all those elaborate interpretations of his novels which take for granted his literary genius. One can only point out the wild incompatibility of those interpretations one with another, suggest that this is due to the lack of achieved meaning in the works themselves, and offer this explanation of that lack.

Of course there are things to praise in Faulkner. In *As I Lay Dying* both the narrative outline and the humour are in the significant sense original; and the book is full of observation. We get a sense of knowing a family and a way of life. Scenes like the wake, and scenes like the crossing of the river, are full of interest and excitement. Everything to do with Anse, and Cash, and Tull, is successful. Anse is one of Faulkner's minor triumphs. He is perhaps the opposite end to Jason Compson in that narrow range of human types whom Faulkner really understands and can sympathise with. Anse's point of view,

'And now I can see same as second sight the rain shutting down betwixt us, a-coming up that road like a durn man, like it wasn't ere a other house to rain on in all the living land. '

is after all a comic version of what Faulkner himself inclines to. But in Darl's and Vardaman's sections especially, and in everything to do with the dead mother, a portentousness is introduced into the book, a significance Faulkner can't handle. If Darl were made simply crazy, and not Quentin Compson in blue jeans; and if Addie had been a plain hard-working woman, and not a protagonist of semi-Lawrentian values; and Whitfield not a comment on the religious life; then it might have been a minor classic. But Faulkner's talent was somehow essentially linked to a desire to exaggerate and falsify, both for himself and others. Thus one critic suggests that this book is 'a fable . . . showing the peculiar precariousness with which Americans meet a common obligation through momentarily concerted action. At any rate Europeans sometimes see in *As I Lay Dying* an example of the unstable moral intensity which drives Americans on rare occasions to a grotesque Quixotic gallantry.'

It was just this readiness to attach enormous significances to the enigmatic which made Faulkner spoil his original idea; and the way the critics have abetted and outdone him makes his current reputation an intellectual disease.

There is very little to praise in *Light in August*, except the way the race theme, embodied in Joe Christmas, recurs throughout the action with a cumulative rhetorical effectiveness; here for once the ambiguity (as to whether he has negro blood) strikes one as artistically justified. But when we are told that the glory of the book is its abundance of representation, when we hear of its superb rendering of country sights and sounds, when it is offered us as the archetypal American novel, what can we think? Only that the critics cannot appreciate description except when the landscape is seen through a haze of heat and dust, and through a distorting exhaustion in the viewer's mind. If we include any other mode of description, we can name a dozen writers who can offer an abundance of representation beside which Faulkner's is meagre indeed. And could anything be more misjudged as fiction, less convincing on any level, less meaningful, than those colloquies between Byron Bunch and Hightower? They are classics of ineptitude.

In *The Sound and the Fury* we have Faulkner's finest achievement, Jason's episode. Jason has, like Anse, that sense that everything is against him which always arouses Faulkner's sympathy; and he has also that sardonic vulgarity and energy of tone which arouses his admiration. Jason is Faulkner's nearest approach to a voice that could express his experience. (It can be compared to the way Basil Seal's voice and career functions for Evelyn Waugh; the authors have their likenesses, in their melancholy misanthropy – though Waugh is much the more talented of the two; and their spokesmen are both exhilaratingly unscrupulous black sheep of noble family.) Faulkner sometimes fails with Jason; he insists on our recognising the limitations of the character, by putting him into situations where something is demanded from him which Faulkner can't give. In the interviews with Caddy about her baby, for instance, one feels the need for some relationship on Jason's part towards his sister, some awareness of her in him, which isn't there. But there is a wonderful variety of scene and mood; the scenes with Uncle Job, the conversation about Babe Ruth; the thoughts of Lorraine; and once, with his mother, there is even a sense of that underside to his nature, that counterpoint to his dominant mood, which is most of the time denied. Jason's view of life is one that Faulkner can render from inside; so that we both recognise it as an oddity and share it as a possibility. But the opposite is true of all the other characters, and when one reads that the book is a blazing work of genius, that it 'presents experience at a level of completeness, fidelity, and significance which is close to high point of possibility in the novel',* one can only think that the critic had suffered some momentary brainstorm.

But in point of fact, of course, this is the consensus of critical opinion; bolstered up by volumes upon volumes of argument and interpretation and comparison. It is the critical opinion of England as well as of America, and even of, perhaps especially of, France. Malraux, Camus, Sartre: French intellectual life at its

*Richard Chase, in *The American Novel and its Tradition*.

most authoritative has stamped Faulkner with an unreserved guarantee – he is the authentic voice of his country. And in America it is not only the Southern writers who have praised him, but those critics we associate more with New York: Irving Howe, Alfred Kazin, Richard Chase. The Southern writers' enthusiasm could be understood, since Faulkner constructed an objective correlative to the sensibility they prescribed in *I'll Take My Stand*; and perhaps the best one can do towards understanding the other critics' remarks is to remind oneself how well Faulkner fitted into the sensibility of Existentialism. Thus we find Alfred Kazin saying, as the climax to a very excited essay, that Joe Christmas's story is 'the search of the "stranger", *l'étranger*, to become man'. Though no intellectual himself, Faulkner was markedly responsive to intellectual atmosphere – Christ-figures start appearing in his novels the moment critics begin talking, or even thinking, about myth and blasphemy; and his lowbrow liking for violence and mystification blandly draped itself in highbrow allusions. But it was even more that the enigmatic portentousness of his manner, the sheer temerity of his performance, his unique blend of significance and unmeaning, make him the perfect material for any kind of explication and propaganda.

His success is, however, a sinister phenomenon. He was, after all, only a minor talent who produced quite major engines of mental torture, crucifixions of literary sensibility; and yet he has been praised, idolised, by fine literary critics of the keenest sensibility. There are likely to be, therefore, powerful forces at work distorting their judgement in his favour. Some of these are merely literary, but even these amount to a suicide of the literary mind; a taste for violence and obscurity so strong as to amount to a distaste – considering the extremeness of the case, this scarcely seems exaggerated

– a distaste for active intelligence and real experience; a zest for 'explication' so strong as to amount to a distaste for clear meaning on the writer's part – and leading to a new kind of critical essay, not really about the book's literary qualities, and not openly about ideas, but sliding from one to the other, and giving the critic a new scope by excusing him his old duties. Others of these forces are more than literary. Thus when Alfred Kazin praises Faulkner we are not at all surprised to find him telling us that the South is the only part of America where one can escape from American bigness, American smoothness, American abstractness, American slogans, the juggernaut of American progress; the anger with one's country is the natural complement of one's love of Joe Christmas. By his sympathetic analysis, the critic participates in Faulkner's depiction of the modern world – appropriates its bitter and destructive insights – identifies himself with its tragic profundity – and elevates himself to the status of social prophet while seeming to praise the truth of Faulkner's artistic vision. The love of Faulkner expresses a hate of America.

Franny and Zooey

The reception given to *Franny and Zooey* in America has illustrated again the interesting paradox of Salinger's reputation there; great public enthusiasm, of the *Time* magazine and Best Seller List kind, accompanied by a repressive coolness in the critical journals. What makes this a paradox is that the book's themes are among the most ambitiously highbrow, and its craftsmanship most uncompromisingly virtuoso. What makes it an interesting one is that those who are most patronising about the book are those who most resemble its characters; people whose ideas and language in their best moments resemble Zooey's. But they feel they ought not to enjoy the book. There is a very strong feeling in American literary circles that Salinger and love of Salinger must be discouraged.

I know from my own experience that *Partisan Review*, a few years ago, rejected an article about him on the grounds that he should not be taken that seriously; and *Commentary*, more recently, declined the offer of an article with the remark that they were, on the contrary, looking for someone to attack him. The paradox is that if you wanted to define the social type of which Zooey Glass is the fictional portrait, you could say 'the readers-of and writers-for *Partisan Review* and

Commentary'. The type certainly exists, and flourishes; it is very prominent in literary circles in America today. And no one denies that the portrait is faithful, and skilful, and vivid. But the originals of the portrait conspire to not-discuss it; so strong is the feeling against his literary mode among them.

That is the way it has been for this last decade. No one has denied that Salinger has talent, but no one has granted that it is major. He is 'one of today's best little writers'. Undergraduates, or at least freshmen, like *The Catcher in the Rye*, but their teachers more often prefer *Nine Stories*. 'For Esmé, with Love and Squalor' is taken as the high point of his achievement. The late stories are the occasion for virtuous variants on 'I'm afraid I just couldn't get through it'.

But one has seen those assured tones before when they have been proved wrong. I met that first phrase in a 1925 review of D. H. Lawrence, which began, 'One of today's best little writers is D. H. Lawrence'. And in fact Lawrence's reputation, for a decade or so, followed a course rather like Salinger's. He was widely read, and enthusiastically discussed, mostly by young people, and as a personality and a dogmatist more than as a writer; but in print, in responsible, even *avant-garde*, journals, it was agreed to consider him a writer for adolescents, not interesting to mature minds, and (at almost any point in his career) going downhill fast. *Sons and Lovers* was looked back to nostalgically, after *Women in Love*, just as *The Catcher in the Rye* is looked back to, today, now we have 'Zooey'. Both writers, it is claimed – and of course it could be true – have an excessive influence on immature minds, with bad effects on their intellectual and moral taste; and responsible people, though they may enjoy the books themselves, should speak coolly of them in public, to induce a sense of proportion. George Steiner's essay, 'The

Salinger Industry', and William York Tindall's book, *D. H. Lawrence and Susan His Cow*, are examples of this attitude taken to the point of aggression. I don't mean to insinuate that Salinger is in any way a similar writer to Lawrence; obviously no two writers could be much more unlike; but the similarity of their treatments should remind us not to take the present critical unanimity against Salinger too seriously. There is the noblest of precedents for ignoring it.

The criticism of Salinger that seems to lie behind this assurance that 'he just isn't that important' is that he writes about and for and out of adolescence. And it is clearly true that Salinger has written more about adolescents and children than he has about adults, and that his writing about them has a specially luminous quality. Those portraits are what one remembers after first reading, because around them, as subjects, the gaiety, the wit, the spontaneity of feeling, the inventiveness of detail, the freshness of taste, all concentrate most. Esmé and Phoebe Caulfield are perhaps the most striking examples of this among the children, Holden and Franny Glass among the adolescents.

Of *Nine Stories* this analysis is true both descriptively and destructively. However often one reads 'Esmé', the second half remains less successful than the first. The scenes involving Sgt X and Clay are as unsuccessful as they are unhappy – and obviously in part *because* they are unhappy, because the adult-world lacks the child-world's chance of happiness. The portraits of adults are rarely as vivid, and never as truly interesting, as those of children; and the contrast between the two (take for instance the contrast between Teddy, in the story of that name, and the odious young man who interviews him) makes one see that luminousness of the children as charged with the intensity of a compulsive recoil from adult life. It is only a brilliant talent one is aware of there, not a major one.

But when we come to *The Catcher in the Rye*, the case is quite different. It is true that what is shown as repulsive in adults, in children is held excusable; that is, that Phoebe – obviously because she is a child – can persecute a little boy who follows her around, and generally 'assert her ego', without involving herself, for Salinger, in the general human ugliness. It is true that, of the two people Holden turns to for help, Phoebe and Mr Antolini, the latter, though the best thing the adult world has to offer, is so discolored and tarnished by his compromises that his advice is invalid. And there are many other such points; the nuns are the only likable adults, *because* they have renounced all forms of self-assertion; Holden likes James Castle, though he had not really known him, *for being* heroically dead; the person he likes best in the Bible, after Jesus, is the lunatic who lived in the tombs and cut himself with stones; he cannot like Romeo because it was in his service, however indirectly, that Mercutio died. Salinger makes it perfectly clear that Holden, and his creator, have an insurmountable, an obsessive, a disqualifying distaste for certain necessary features of the human condition. We are all under the necessity of breathing air, taking up space, eating food, seeking love, wielding power, which other people might conceivably want or need; and of still remaining on speaking terms with ourselves. Holden, and Salinger, cannot get over this.

But this is a criticism of Salinger (though after all the same is true of some quite major writers) without being a criticism of the book. Because what Holden thinks is only part of what he does, and that total is something vigorous and formidable; not restricted by that obsessive patterning of experience we find in the stories, not marred by that cramping insistence on fragility, pain, defeat. The inadequacy of the advice the adult world has to offer Holden, and the ugliness of the way it acts towards him, are less important than the way he acts towards it. Holden is not a victim. In every encounter in the book he comes off the victor, in the simplest sense, by the most empirical standards. He is *stronger* than Carl Luce, Mr Antolini, Mrs Morrow, Mr Spencer, the girls from Seattle. Our private sympathies, invested in him, find themselves vindicated time and time again; *successful*. Holden is not just a sensitive adolescent; nor even just an intelligent and energetic adolescent, as Franny is; he is a mode of action, a way of solving (though not a solution) of the problems the book has set up. Obviously these problems – the overbearing ugliness of the world and human nature – remain a large part of the book. But, and this is the point, Holden's way of acting is a larger part, and consequently the problems he faces do not have the same significance as they did in the world of *Nine Stories*. Holden is not an ordinary kind of character in the book; no more is Kostya Levin, in *Anna Karenina*, but Salinger's hero is even more special in his function than Tolstoy's, as I shall try to show at the end of the chapter.

When we come to the Glass family stories, this charge, that Salinger can write only about and for adolescents, becomes demonstrably false. Not because the characters are older, and even Franny is twenty; I would grant that in the description of her crying in 'Franny', and of her waking up in 'Zooey', we find the same fragile prettiness of detail, the same fond fearfulness of tone, as limits the value of so many affirmative portraits in *Nine Stories*. Nor because of Seymour and Buddy, in the treatment of whom there is plenty of detail that could be argued either way; some things are more romantically self-indulgent than the worst of *Nine Stories*. But because, in this volume and in the other two late stories, 'Raise High the Roofbeam, Car-penters', and 'Introducing Seymour', the major success is clearly Zooey. And while Zooey has his problems with 'being mature', there is surely no point in calling him an adolescent. Only a quite special theory of the American writer and his maturity could find the writing about him immature. Zooey is in fact as special a kind of creation as Holden, and cannot be judged simply as a character; but in so far as he is a realistic portrait – which is to say, quite magnificently – it is of a very complicated and committed adult.

It is the magnificence one must come back to, for it is only the fact that Salinger is a major artist that makes these quarrels over the meaning of 'adolescence' significant. Not that because he is so accomplished he deserves special scrupulousness of treatment – a specially precise use of descriptive categories – but that his greatness *is* the extra range of his meanings. He handles adolescent situations and emotions with an imagination which makes them *fully* significant to adults – with the same kind of significance as adult situations and emotions have. The success – that is, the perfection – of the scene between Holden and Phoebe, is that it is not only a lifelike conversation between an adolescent and his sister, and not only beautiful, touching, amusing, in its lifelikeness; but that it is also two people very gifted for life being as serious with each other as they can be – being more serious than most people ever manage. That is what commands such fullness of attention in us. Because this level of reality is just as convincingly rendered as the others, Salinger is *both* – they are two ways of saying the same thing – *not* writing for adolescents, *and* a major artist.

In *The Catcher in the Rye* Salinger established himself as a great realist; and it is perhaps because we have forgotten what realism is that we have failed to recognise his achievement. It has been the great discovery of modern literature that fiction need not be realistic; James, Lawrence, Joyce, Proust, none of them achieved his best effects by describing people and events so as to convince the reader that they literally happened just like that, in some other literal time and place. Great reputations, like Faulkner's, have been granted to ambitious attempts to do something non-realistic in fiction; great novelists of the past have been re-assessed and re-interpreted in order to show that they were not mere realists. Consequently, we tend to assume that all there is to realism in dialogue, for instance, is that every remark in *The Catcher in the Rye* shall have the ring of the New York idiom. We forget that realism also captures the multiplicity of that idiom – its difference and yet sameness in Carl Luce and the cab-drivers, its liveliness in Holden, its deadness in Maurice – and so, with marvellous economy, calls up the whole city before us. We forget that realism also means the rendering of places and events of all kinds, public and private; and behaviour of all kinds, in individuals and groups; and since it applies most strictly of all to a narrator's own style, all this has to be achieved without overt effort or even intention. It is just this realism which makes the book so much more distinguished than *Nine Stories*. The wider, soberer, more impersonal ambition – to record, and render, the whole city; and the severer discipline – the renunciation of all descriptive adjectives and prophetic epiphanies; these purge away the too-insistent lyricism and portentousness of the early work. All the more personal concerns are sacrificed to authenticity, to probability turned into an artistic virtue.

In the Glass family stories, the writer has to convince us of the authenticity, the probability, of the idiom of a group of people who are by definition improbable, especially in their speech. He reports them, moreover, in bizarre situations, and weaves in allusions to a most complicated and implausible family history. Who for instance could have any standard to judge the authenticity of the way a young man like Zooey would talk to his mother (such a mother) in his bath while his sister was undergoing a religious experience in the living-room? And yet who is not convinced of the truth of all the crowded detail, as true not only to the individual, and to the family member, but also to the citizen – though eccentric – of that part of New York in that part of the decade?

If *The Catcher in the Rye* is realism, this is super-realism. The novel, both in its individual sentences and in its total form, is virtually unfaultable in seeming to be what it claims to be, a first-person, seventeen-year-old narrative. All its complicated and qualified meanings are filtered through this narrow mesh, for the sake, most obviously, of authority of illusion and immediacy of response. In the later stories the narrator admits to being a professional writer, which seems to make Holden's kind of 'sincerity' impossible, and yet Buddy achieves an equal immediacy, by a series of technical devices of progressive and finally fantastic difficulty. In 'Zooey', for instance, the narrator 'betrays' a personal involvement above all in his description of the characters; by a direct affectionateness, a fantasticality of phrase, an almost total visual blur; and in the introduction, by a fatal cleverness, a squirming self-consciousness and over-writing, which guarantee the non-professional, exceptional character of *this* story. In 'Introducing Seymour' the bad writing is not merely peripheral, but central, and Salinger offers to convince us, by his failures – his hysteria of phrase, discontinuity of structure, embarrassing intimacy and swerves of tone and so on – that he has something to say so powerful, so disturbing, that he can't write well. In fact, being an honest craftsman, he claims at the end to have conveyed that meaning, to have 'given us Seymour'; more by his failure to make us see him or understand him than by his success.

There has been a comparable development, from realism to super-realism, in every aspect of Salinger's art. In the evocation of places, for instance, the novel describes typical New York settings with a dazzling economy of detail; Ernie's nightclub is evoked almost entirely by the closeness of the tables and the conversations at them. In 'Zooey', on the other hand, there are no typical localities, and the detail is part fantastic; for instance, the 'host of golden pharmaceuticals' in the medicine cabinet, and the 'visual hymn to commercial American childhood and early puberty' on the living-room walls.

In the novel there is a predominance of representative events – the afternoon at the theatre, the Rockettes, the talks with cab-drivers, and with the prostitute. Others, like the meeting with the nuns, are not merely representative just because they are so much the result of Holden's unusual strengths. And of course the talk with Phoebe takes place in a wholly private, wholly free world, where only strengths are engaged. The incidents in the late stories are nearly *all* of this last kind; they are between members of the Glass family; they take place in a private world. Those that involve outside reality often have a character of the fantastic and farcical, like the first half of 'Raise High the Roof-beam, Carpenters'.

In *The Catcher in the Rye* the range of intellectual and aesthetic reference is severely limited to the personal and colloquial. Holden likes the books that make you 'wish you could call the author up on the phone whenever you felt like it', and he thinks 'old Jesus' would never have sent Judas to Hell. In the Glass family stories Socrates and Jesus, Kafka and Kierkegaard, Zen Buddhism and Christian mysticism are invoked on every page. Conflicts between people are defined in terms of such ideas, and the major themes all derive from a conscious struggle between the worldly life and a purely religious idealism.

In the novel, finally, all the characters but one are representative; even someone as relatively internalised as Mr Antolini represents a social and intellectual type. In the late stories everyone is of the stature of that one exception, Holden himself. Zooey, Franny, Buddy, even Bessie, they are all exceptional people, and in the same style as Holden. By the power of their personalities, and by the way they relate to each other, they permit Salinger's kind of truth to be told, and his kind of feelings to be expressed, his kind of life to be lived. They constitute a myth world; in two senses, with two consequences. They so completely embody and characterise significant reality, relevant standards, for each other, that between them there is a private space – in physical terms, the parents' apartment – where their problems can be worked out relatively unhampered, their energies freed from the struggle with the outside world. And they so completely transcend the limits of their individual stories, even of fictional characters – in literal terms, by the quantity and complexity of detail about them – that they create that private area in the reading public's mind, too.

That is, the insistence on their public as well as private careers – the national eminence of Zooey's acting and Seymour's poetry – and the assurance of so many stories about them still to come, make us say to ourselves 'Salinger really wants us to believe there really are such people'. This is super-realism in characterisation. Holden also transcends the limits of his book, and also achieves a private freedom with Phoebe, but the contrast is clear.

By this means, working in this mode, Salinger is able to tackle more ambitious themes and to achieve more brilliant effects. Take for instance the structure of 'Zooey', with its extreme paucity of action and lengthiness of argument and the overwhelming effect Salinger gets out of it. Or take the stylistic virtuosity of the same story. All the four characters have the same highly idiosyncratic style of talk. Even Bessie's remarks (about Waker: 'He's so sentimental. If you tell Waker it looks like rain his eyes fill up'; about Les: 'He thinks anything peculiar or unpleasant will just go away if he turns on the radio and some little schnook starts singing') could almost be spoken by Zooey. And yet every remark can be attributed, on quite internal evidence, to its speaker. One can even recognise the relatedness of Buddy's three styles – in the letter, on the 'phone, in the introduction. The total style, more-over, the style of the whole story, including not only the different idioms, but the differences between them, including the virtuosity, this is itself a part of the meaning; for it is a powerful assertion of vitality, of gaiety, humour, delight in the detail and process of existence, which quite determines the balance for us between the life-praising and life-denying elements of the argument. The old weaknesses of Salinger's temperament are turned into strengths by this quite technical manœuvre.

Moreover, that part of Salinger's late work which is not in this mode is much less successful; it begins to suffer from the old weaknesses. 'Franny' is much more like *Nine Stories* in event and setting and cast of characters. Franny has to formulate her ideas away from home and family, in a 'typical' setting and occasion; neither style nor incident achieve the colour and comic energy of 'Raise High the Roofbeam, Carpenters'; even the religious exposition lacks the glamour of epigram and famous name it has in the other stories; the private Glass world, the myth, does not protect and support the theme. And consequently the story is thin and unconvincing in the old ways. One does not *see* Lane, one does not dislike him as much as the author does, one does not assent very fully to the latter's evaluation of the crisis. The pattern of experience, the kind of sensibility, which the story renders, is one in which there is too sharp a cleavage between the sensitive and the brutal, where the innocent are *too* innocent, and the Philistine *too* Philistine. One does not believe, in fact, that Lane would reply, four or five times running, only in comments on food while Franny – so obviously, so melodramatically, upset – was expounding the life of the Pilgrim. One feels something wrong when one contrasts these two sentences: 'Lane put his fingers – which were slender and long, and usually not far out of sight – around the stem of his glass . . . Her extended fingers, though trembling, or because they were trembling, looked oddly graceful and pretty.' What one feels is a pressure in the writer's mind, to attack one and protect the other, an obsessive, distorting pressure, a bruise of the sensibility. The portrait of Lane is very like that of the young man in 'Teddy'. Unsustained by the techniques of either realism or super-realism, Salinger's art again shows too easy and mechanical an expectation of defeat for the good and victory for the bad, too simple, too sentimental an emotion for and against his characters.

But Salinger's most important technical invention is not a matter of either realism or super-realism. He has solved his own problems as a writer and opened new worlds to other writers, mostly by means of a new kind of character. On the whole, character, like realism, has been at a discount in modern fiction, and Salinger's bold experiments in it are responsible for much of the irritation at the later stories. People complain that after all there *is* no such person as Seymour Glass, or that after all Buddy Glass *is* Salinger himself. But the really major success in character is achieved only twice, in Zooey and Holden.

We may perhaps call Buddy a first-person and Seymour a second-person character. Salinger, that is, gives Buddy an expression rather like that of a photographer's snap of himself taking a photograph; half silly grin and half busy abstraction. Seymour is the other half of an I–Thou dialogue; never fully seen, never really convincing or sympathetic. Zooey and Holden are fully rounded third-person characters, but of no normal kind. They are characters who are larger than their creator.

They are, that is, more intelligent, more vigorous, more gifted, in exactly the ways that compensate for Salinger's weaknesses; and they bulk so large in the worlds in which they appear that they create a new balance, a new order in the writer's meaning. If Holden, that is, did not exceed his bounds as a character, escape his limits as only part of his creator's mind, the novel would only be a longer 'De Daumier-Smith'. The structure of the book, after all, announces the boy's defeat; it is only the force of his personality that makes us remember the episodes as a kind of victory. If Zooey's personality did not crowd out even Seymour's, his story would be only a longer 'Franny'. It is partly what Zooey actually thinks and says. The kind of irritation he feels at Franny, and Buddy, and Seymour ('this goddam house is lousy with smilers') is after all both convincing and crucial; it is exactly the criticism of Salinger's religiosity one has felt oneself.

But it is even more that the very pitch and rhythm of Zooey's personality, whatever he is saying, is an effective antidote to the too lyrical, too emotional, too complacently disintegrate tones of Franny and Buddy. Salinger has not merely built self-criticism into a story, he has let it take over.

In the ways they 'take over' their respective stories, Holden and Zooey are different. Zooey is an anti-body in his creator's mind, a Devil's Advocate, a conscious critic and opponent of congenital tendencies and attitudes. Holden is the embodiment of all that Salinger delights in and fears for; it is only in the power of his personality and his place in the novel that he denies his creator's categories. But to both of them the writer surrenders part of his most personal intentions, his most confirmed habitual meanings. Zooey and Holden are allowed to resist, to correct, the categories of the imaginative worlds in which they appear. As such they are a uniquely interesting literary phenomenon. As such, also, they help create two of the half-dozen superb works of literature of our generation. I can compare them, for vitality, only to Tolstoy's two autobiographical heroes, Kostya Levin and Pierre Bezukhov. This is of course a very ambitious comparison. Tolstoy is a novelist of much greater scope than Salinger; and his heroes have a solidity, a variety of reality, which we miss in Holden and Zooey. But in this matter of a character's autonomy, independent life, power to outreach his creator, I really think Salinger's the more brilliant achievement.

American Rococo:

Salinger and Nabokov

‘ *Nous connûmes* (this is royal fun) the would-be enticements of their repetitious names – all those Sunset Motels, U-Beam Cottages, Hillcrest Courts, Pine View Courts, Mountain View Courts, Skyline Courts, Park Plaza Courts, Green Acres, Mac's Courts. There was sometimes a special line in the write-up, such as "Children welcome, pets allowed" (*You* are welcome, *you* are allowed). The baths were mostly tiled showers, with an endless variety of spouting mechanisms, but with one definitely non-Laodicean characteristic in common, a propensity, while in use, to turn instantly beastly hot or blindingly cold upon you, depending on whether your neighbor turned on his cold or his hot to deprive you of a necessary complement in the shower you had so carefully blended. Some motels had instructions pasted above the toilet (on whose tank the towels were unhygienically heaped) asking guests not to throw into its bowl garbage, beer cans, cartons, stillborn babies; others had special notices under glass, such as Things to Do (Riding: *You will often see riders coming down Main Street on their way back from a romantic moonlight ride.* "Often at 3 am.", sneered unromantic Lo.) ’

‘ Franny Glass lay asleep on the couch, with an afghan over her; the "wall-to-wall" carpet had neither been taken up nor folded in at the corners; and the furniture – seemingly, a small warehouse of it – was in its usual static-dynamic distribution. The room was not impressively large, even by Manhattan apartment-house standards, but its accumulated furnishings might have lent a snug appearance to a banqueting hall in Valhalla. There was a Steinway grand piano (invariably kept open), three radios (a 1927 Freshman, a 1932 Stromberg–Carlson, and a 1941 RCA) a twenty-one-inch-screen television set, four table-model phonographs (including a 1920 Victrola, with its speaker still mounted intact, topside), cigarette and magazine tables galore, a regulation-size ping-pong table (mercifully collapsed and stored behind the piano), four comfortable chairs, eight uncomfortable chairs, a twelve-gallon tropical-fish tank (filled to capacity, in every sense of the word, and illuminated by two forty-watt bulbs), a love seat, the couch Franny was occupying, two empty bird cages, a cherrywood writing table, and an assortment of floor lamps, table lamps, and "bridge" lamps that sprang up all over the congested inscape like sumac.   '

These two passages, though obviously enough by different writers, are in the same style. This is a style characterised by its exuberant and recondite vocabulary, highly literary and highly technical at the same time, lavish of foreign phrases, commercial terms, academic turns of speech. It is always elaborate, sometimes formal, in its phrasing and sentence-structure, but far from pompous; indeed, its outspoken desire to perform, to be entertaining and be entertained, makes it at first sight undignified. Its images are extremely clever, its manner consistently self-conscious, its effects all variations on a theme of exaggeration.

The sentences are crowded with allusions to phenomena specific to the present day and one country – names we meet in the world of serious imagination with some shock of surprise – and the tone of these allusions is satiric but poetic. The objects named become colourful, intricate, attractive; but they are bathed in a tricky, treacherous light, shot with viridian and gamboge; most unlike the broad shafts of sunlight bathing the broad and noble cornfields in ordinary poetic descriptions of America. The tones of this style as a whole are tricky; remarkably vivid and varied, and unstable, in their self-consciousness and readiness to change. The events are narrated by a very personal and self-exposing 'I'; to a degree that we realise is a device, a part of some impersonal strategy; but as we penetrate *that* strategy, the writing becomes again unusually personal—nakedly emotional, frankly disturbed.

As we read the book as a whole, we find that the sensibility expressed in the style expresses itself also in a battery of structural devices; if the style is the fingers which actually touch and grasp and manipulate, then the book is engineered like a pair of arms to subserve that functioning. The personal tone turns out to be an elaborate self-portrait of a narrator; and the total figure of that narrator mediates between the author and his meaning just as his particular metaphors and phrasings do. There is a plethora of narrative devices – forewords, footnotes, letters, reminiscences, speeches – each with its own individual manner; which build up to massive proportions, to critical mass, the stylistic virtuosity of the book. Effects of time and space are drastically diminished and expanded; the camera is brought up so close sometimes (to Lolita, say, or to Bessie Glass) that every feature is hugely blurred. And in the events and characters themselves there is the same mingling of the fantastic and the diurnal as in the prose. The large structural features express, enact, the same sensibility.

Also, as we read the book as a whole, we find that the themes and subject-matter express this same sensibility, in some ways. Not in all ways, just as the writers' use of language is not always what we have described; they have soberer, tenderer, uglier, more violent things to say from time to time. But an important part of their subject-matter and meaning fits into this style as into a glove; demands it. Let us look at another pair of passages.

‘Sweet hot jazz, square dancing, gooey fudge sundaes, musicals, movie magazines and so forth – these were the obvious items in her list of beloved things. The Lord knows how many nickels I fed to the gorgeous music boxes that came with every meal we had! I still hear the nasal voices of those invisibles serenading her, people with names like Sammy and Jo and Eddy and Tony and Peggy and Guy and Patty and Rex, and sentimental song hits, all of them as similar to my ear as her various candies were to my palate. She believed, with a kind of celestial trust, any advertisement or advice that appeared in *Movie Love* or *Screen Land* – Starasil Starves Pimples, or "You better watch out if you're wearing your shirt-tails outside your jeans, gals, because Jill says you shouldn't". If a roadside sign said VISIT OUR GIFT SHOP – we *had* to visit it, *had* to buy its Indian curios, dolls, copper jewelry, cactus candy. The words "novelties and souvenirs" simply entranced her by their trochaic lilt. If some café sign proclaimed Icecold Drinks, she was automatically stirred, although all drinks everywhere were icecold.   ’

‘Will you be content with that standard box-office schmalz? Or will you dream of something more cosmic – zum Beispiel, playing Pierre or Andrey in a Technicolor production of War and Peace, with stunning battlefield scenes, and all the nuances of characterisation left out (on the grounds that they're novelistic and unphotogenic), and Anna Magnani daringly cast as Natasha (just to keep the production classy and Honest), and gorgeous incidental music by Dmitri Popkin, and all the male leads intermittently rippling their jaw muscles to show they're under great emotional stress, and a World Première at the Winter Garden, under floodlights, with Molotov and Milton Berle and Governor Dewey introducing the celebrities as they come into the theatre. (By celebrities I mean, of course, old Tolstoy-lovers – Senator Dirksen, Zsa Zsa Gabor, Gayelord Hauser, Georgie Jessel, Charles of the Ritz.) How does that sound?   ’

Here again we have catalogues of modern American

phenomena. The tone is in a sense the opposite of that of Whitman's catalogues; the writers are proclaiming not the fitness but the unfitness of these objects to be the adjuncts of the good life. Nevertheless, the effect is not to communicate the disgust the writers say they are feeling. What *we* feel, as we read, is a delighted recognition. Named in this way, these objects, our environment, becomes funny, vivid, glamorous, touching. This *is* a kind of yea-saying, though very different from the kind Whitman aimed at. The things named may be of any emotional colour, but all colours are bright, all the flavours are piquant, and the dominant mood is of reckless holiday.

The things named are moreover made real. They are not specified merely to identify and justify an emotion in the speaker (as they sometimes are in Faulkner's descriptions, for example) but for their own sake. This style serves, among other things, a kind of realism, a word we have almost forgotten. It reminds us how powerful and various a mode that can be. A reader doesn't respond to realistic writing with merely an approving nod ('Good work, a boy like that *would* reply like that') but with any one or any blending of a dozen strong feelings. This would be clearer if we had quoted passages of dialogue; Holden Caulfield and Lolita, in their different ways, get wonderfully varied effects out of American adolescent slang; we are amused, amazed, deeply moved, merely by recognising the language we hear around us every day. (The characters also are realistic – we are asked to believe in them more literally and manifoldly than in, say, Faulkner's characters – but that is not so much to the point here.) These writers are passionately interested in what their characters eat, wear, and hum, as well as what they dream, dread, and aspire to. Their books are importantly about America.

This realism is so unlike the Zolaesque variety that has set its stamp on the whole mode, however, that we must find some other term to qualify it. Far from stressing the sordid and nasty in their descriptions, Salinger avoids them, Nabokov transforms them; it is the picturesque and pretty they emphasise. Far from stressing the material limitations, the animalities, of the human condition, they emphasise its gaieties and elegancies. (This is a paradox, about *Lolita*, of course; but the book itself is a paradox, from this point of view; Nabokov is working equally hard at opposite effects.) This realism, despite its criticalness, its exasperation, its recurrent disgust, despite the inner convulsions and destructiveness of the writers, is a kind of affirmation of the American scene and of the possibilities of life in America. But it is a rococo affirmation, playful, orna-mental, lyrical, precarious; the style is a kind of American rococo.

These likenesses between two writers, this participation in a common style, is more than a coincidence. Although their interests (and their weaknesses) as novelists are so different, for each of them the discovery of this manner has meant the release of their best powers and the achievement of their best writing. Indeed, it is more than that, for the problems this manner solves (the cul-de-sacs it avoids) were more than individual, and its discovery means something to all of us.

Those problems are sufficiently indicated if we remind ourselves of some of the labels our era has given itself. Ours is the Age of Alienation, in which all seriously imaginative people have felt themselves out of place, and the time out of joint. The *Esquire* literary conferences have been especially full of this kind of feeling – 'Life in America in 1960 is hell', said John Cheever at one of them, and people like Philip Roth and James Baldwin agreed; for of all twentieth-century countries America has seemed the most alien. Ours is also the Age of Anxiety, in which all imaginative people have felt profoundly unhappy about the human condition as such; in its humbler forms this includes a habitual recourse to psychoanalysis, and a nagging guilt about being an intellectual. And there are other labels, indicating sufficiently different things, but things which cohere and support each other, and even feed each other. There is a profound unhappiness about the conditions of life anywhere, anytime, sharpening to a climax in reference to the here and now and the sensitive, serious 'I'.

Something went wrong in history – with the Industrial Revolution, or with the Reformation, or with the Renaissance, or with the Fall of Man – and in our day the pace of decay is accelerating feverishly. Every specifically modern feature, every new development – supermarkets, drive-in-cinemas, motels – must be a lurch further into alienation.

This is one of the hidden sources of the anti-Americanism among intellectuals, in America as much as in Europe. Since the West is going in fundamentally the wrong direction, the country furthest ahead must be the furthest astray, the places where the past still lingers must be the healthiest, and any pride or pleasure taken in 'progress' must be the crudest, crassest self-delusion. Cultural health is identified with medieval faith-plus-feudalism; or with the apprentice-jostling-courtier audience at Shakespeare's 'Globe'; and any artifact or detail of theirs, any model or groundplan of a monastery or a theatre, brings to mind the fundamental inter-relatedness of their lives – art, religion, labour, and birth, marriage, death, all interwoven in one gorgeous tapestry. But advertising signs, radios, TV, super-highways, movies, all these bring to mind

the impoverishment and disconnectedness and unsatis-
fyingness of living under modern conditions.

We were brought up to believe these things (it's
embarrassing now to *say* them – because they have
become credal) and I'm not ready to say I disbelieve
them. But the mood they dictate cannot, any more than
any other mood, continue indefinitely to interest and
inspire and satisfy; after a time it no longer explains
our deepest feelings, or results in our sharpest thinking;
it becomes not only embarrassing to say these things,
but boring.

There are signs that that time has now passed. Those
signs include, in literary matters, the withdrawal into
silence of the New Critics, and the decline in production and reputation of the Southern Gothic school.
There is a multitude of other signs, in magazines and
quarterlies especially, of a return to common-sense, to
short-term views, and a tentative preference for ideas
that contradict the old ones. It is not the realisation
that modern man is an exile, an outsider, but the ways
he can make himself at home in the here and now; it is
not the acknowledgement of a horror, nightmare, and
dissonance at the source of life, but the possibility of
some harmony and contentment and beauty that are
neither dishonest nor sentimental; it is not the explora-
tion of the difficult, the stark, or the grotesque, in
thought or expression, but the delighted celebration of
the specifically contemporary; these and not those are
likely to characterise the writer or painter or talker who
engages our keenest interest.

This returns us, of course, to Salinger and Nabokov,
and to the way of escape they have discovered from the
old mood. It is an escape because they are still importantly under the dominance of that mood, as we all
must be. The stylistic analysis we have offered would
not do as even the sketchiest account of either writer's

total production. But it does cover the greatest successes, and the parts of each it omits are also relevant to our argument in their own way. For in the last third of *Lolita*, where we are asked to take tragically and grotesquely what we had taken comically and fantastically, and in those parts of Salinger's work where he deals with Seymour Glass, each is a writer of the Age of Alienation. In these sections Salinger and Nabokov present themselves as anguished past endurance by the condition life imposes on man; as unable to accept the nature of human existence and human relations; and in these sections they are less successful artistically. These are great transitional writers, aiming often (perhaps when they are most serious) at phoenix targets set up for them by the prophets of their youth, but deflected by the shifting winds of artistic instinct to bring down running deer, less imposing to them perhaps, but far more beautiful to us. It is only when Salinger and Nabokov are recording most vividly and variously the detail of contemporary life, when they are responding most freely and high-spiritedly to the conditions *that* life imposes on one, when they are creating large-scale characters who enjoy and succeed under those conditions, that they become really magnificent artists.

This is clear when you read any other book by Nabokov, but it is specially easy to compare *Lolita* with *Laughter in the Dark*. In the latter novel also the central character falls in love with a much younger girl – she is 17 but every description stresses her physical immaturity; he loves her desperately, unreciprocated, and she treats him cruelly; he loses her, by treachery, to an ultra-sophisticated and sinister aesthete; and in the end he seeks his revenge with a gun, and himself dies. The situations, characters, and themes are strikingly the same as those of *Lolita*, but this is a fairly typical well-written, sexually perverse, railway-reading novel of the 'thirties. What makes *Lolita* so much more than that is conveyed in those new techniques I have called rococo realism. The first-person narration, the profusion of character detail about Lolita, the passionate interest in the contemporary, the elaborate brilliance of both style and structure, the irresponsible rush of invention and delighted appreciation of anything and everything, in despite of the horror and madness that also has to be written down; by these means Nabokov makes out of that same unpleasant and unpromising material those masses of gaiety and brilliance and intelligence.

In 'A Perfect Day for Bananafish' and even in 'Franny', Salinger deals unsuccessfully with exactly the characters and situations which in 'Zooey' are so perfectly rendered. The omniscient author, the impersonal prose, the neat characterisation, the severe control and limitation of detail to what is relevant to the story's point, its mood; all this has the effect of exposing Salinger's weaknesses, his predilection for defeat and suffering, his too habitual expectation of disaster for the innocent and beautiful, triumph for the brutal and philistine. This predilection, this habit, cramp his invention, his observation, his intelligence; they give us something predictable, almost conventional. In 'Zooey' the hypersensitiveness is intricately interwoven with gaiety, energy, and cleverness; introduced into the story by the first-person narration, the profusion of character detail, the passionate interest in the contemporary; and 'Zooey' is brilliantly successful.

It may be objected that *The Catcher in the Rye* is successful Salinger without particularly fitting this pattern; neither its style nor its structure are as elaborate as those we have analysed. Nevertheless, it owes its success to those elements of rococo realism it does embody. It is the sustained virtuosity and in a sense extravagance of the use of language and the form which makes it so much more impressive than, say, 'Teddy'. It is because so much of New York life is recorded, not for our condemnation, as in 'Uncle Wiggily in Connecticut', but for our appreciative recognition, that our attention is richly engaged. Above all, it is because the personality of Holden Caulfield bulks so large in the novel that we don't feel, as we do in *Nine Stories*, that Salinger is cramped in his response to life. Narrate those same incidents in the third person, with an ordinary-sized character, and their effect would be infinitely more depressing, less rich, less interesting. Ideologically, in a sense, Salinger cheats; he makes Holden's charm and personality irrelevantly important, out of proportion to the size any one person could have in a view of life; and Holden's passing accidental pleasures in things are allowed to counterbalance for us Salinger's sense of their essential inadequacy. Ideologically, then, he cheats; but aesthetically, he wins every prize by the manœuvre. Again the introduction of certain techniques, and the meanings they serve, has demonstrably redeemed the material and the talent.

But the problem, and its solution, are not merely technical, in the limited sense. They have to do with important subject matters and modes of feeling, which concern every imaginative person at one time or another. That is why what Salinger and Nabokov have achieved is so interesting.

Let us return for a moment to the Age of Alienation. As a symbol of all that is most alienating in our culture we can take Hollywood. In the forty years that movies have been a social phenomenon, what writer of any distinction has said anything in their favour? Not the Aldous Huxley novelist, depicting levels of taste. Much less the Dos Passos novelist or the Auden–Spender poet, eager to awaken the working class. Least of all the cultural conservative, from Evelyn Waugh to Allen Tate, concerned for orthodoxy and tradition. The cinema has appeared in the work of all these people under quite remarkably the same aspect, as the gaudy palace of cheap dreams, the factory of mass-produced illusion, the pseudo-Aztec temple of vulgarity, nonsense, and escape. Even the catalogue poets have rarely included the cinema among the things they have so lavishly said 'yes' to.

To that kind of criticism, of course, one finds easy enough answers (there are other aspects of the cinema; and anyway you are out of date about films); but the best marksmen in the cultural phalanx have more interesting things to say. Here is T. S. Eliot:

> ‘ With the decay of the music-hall, with the encroachment of the cheap and rapid-breeding cinema, the lower classes will tend to drop into the same state of protoplasm as the bourgeoisie. The working man who went to the music-hall and saw Marie Lloyd and joined in the chorus was himself performing part of the act; he was engaged in that collaboration of the audience with the artist which is necessary in all art and most obviously in dramatic art. He will now go to the cinema, where his mind is lulled by continuous senseless music and continuous action too rapid for the brain to act upon, and will receive, without giving, in that same listless apathy with which the middle and upper classes regard any entertainment of the nature of art. ’

Here the quality of the film is unimportant, and it is the passivity inherent in all watching which is indicted. This gathers strength from its agreement with many other attacks on the whole trend of modern culture towards passive, anonymous, irresponsible receptivity; we may take Huxley's *Brave New World* as an example of a general survey, and *Lady Chatterley's Lover* for a particular case, where Sir Clifford is shown growing content to be absorbed in his radio. Both D. H. Lawrence and T. S. Eliot, in one of their rare agreements, have wanted a return to communal, participative entertainment and art; and their cry has been taken up by nearly every culture critic of the century, finding its way into nearly every education manual.

Lawrence pushed his analysis further. Alvina Houghton, in *The Lost Girl*, explains to Mr May, who is reluctantly converting his theatre into a cinema, why his working-class audience prefers films.

‘ "The film is only pictures, like pictures in the *Daily Mirror*. And pictures don't have any feelings apart from their own feelings. I mean the feelings of the people who watch them. And that's why they like them. Because they make them feel that they are everything . . . It's because they can spread themselves over a film, and they *can't* over a living performer. They're up against the performer himself. And they hate it . . . You're not up to the mark as they are."

"Not up to the mark? What do you mean? Do you mean they are more intelligent?"

"No, but they're more modern. You like things that aren't yourself. But they don't. They hate to admire anything that they can't take to themselves." ’

This goes further than Eliot's analysis because it draws strength from Lawrence's general diagnosis of modern man's predicament, our deep uneasiness, our too-quick irritation, with physical work, with other people's bodies, with our own; our preference for shapes, shadows, ideas, machines. Defences, counter-arguments, spring to mind; but our purpose is only to recall the original forms, the high authority, the prophetic context, of that prejudice against movies we now take as a part of the nature of things. We can note especially the direction of history. Both Lawrence and Eliot, major prophets of the Age of Alienation, assume that progress is decay – the resentful audience is more *modern* than the theatre-owner, and the working class will now go the way the upper classes *long since* went. The cinema symbolises all that is most advanced and therefore most corrupt.

Salinger and Nabokov offer no contradictions of all this. Indeed their statements are enthusiastically in accord with it. But the attitude they communicate, the effective meaning of those statements, are very different. Let us take Holden Caulfield's description of the movie he sees in Radio City Music Hall. He ends his description: 'All I can say is, don't see it if you don't want to puke all over yourself', and there is no reason to doubt his sincerity or Salinger's agreement with him. But for the reader the description is wholly enjoyable, and it is not approval of satire we feel but delighted recognition; recognition not only of the film but of Holden's performance; for the re-narration of bad films is a major modern conversational resource. After his humiliation by Maurice, the hotel elevator man, Holden pretends to himself that he has been shot, and acts out to himself a gangster movie sequence. Again his comment is: 'The goddam movies. They can ruin you. I'm not kidding', and again Salinger means us to believe him; but what the reader feels is that writer and character have got a great deal of *profit* out of the movies. Holden isn't in the least ruined by them, that we can see; what we see is how useful he finds them in recognising and satirising, *understanding*, his own impulses.

In such passages we recognise the movies as they really appear in our lives, not in the melodramatic rôle they are so often cast for. Intelligent people enjoy and use Hollywood, culturally feed on it, in a dozen ways;

some of which are particularly relevant to our present argument. We enjoy just going to the movies; it's an activity much more easy and natural and normal than going to the theatre; it puts us in the right relation to our neighbour; it confirms in us our rights as twentieth-century citizen, not as aesthete or man-about-town. We enjoy their acute but innocent recordings of our environment. I don't mean in professionally sharp-eyed pieces – let us take the good films for granted and concentrate on average Hollywood products: it can be merely the view of a four-lane highway in a blank Michigan landscape, and a truck speeding along it on a dull afternoon, and the way it slows down to turn into a gas-station, and the array of bright stickers on the office window, and the way the old man hustles out to the pump. This humble but satisfying kind of realism, with no portentous meanings attached, is an art experience we go to Hollywood for. Then the star-system offers us a company of enormous and garish demigods to share with our neighbours; we know their vital statistics, their sexual history, their intellectual ambitions, in implausible but poetically lavish detail; and we watch Shirley Maclaine being this time a Parisian prostitute, next time a Lesbian schoolteacher, with a sympathy and interest – and scepticism – which it would be impossible to maintain in a theatre. For above all what we find in the movies is a certain kind of performer. We can't take Marlon Brando as an example because his performances are often of a somewhat different kind; more vividly mimetic in detail, more deeply brooding in spirit. Marilyn Monroe would do, but her talent, though pure, was slender. Let us take Frank Sinatra; scarcely an actor, much of the time; a vaudeville performer, doing his act, walking into and out of his rôle, or rather standing around in it when he isn't interested; always, deep down, casual and urbane in his relation to his audience. There is a purity of intelligence and feeling in that casualness, a fine calculation of ends and means; and when he *is* interested in the part (I am thinking of films like *Some Came Running*, especially, or *A Hole in the Head*) he achieves a purity of mere male humanity, a fine dry cool unselfconscious poignancy of merely living; a humanity undistinguished by strength or talent, much less integrity, merely more alive than other people, less self-deceiving and self-ashamed, more aware of the possibilities and limitations of life. This is the characteristic Hollywood style and quality, and it corresponds of course to the nonchalance and unpretentiousness of the act of going to the movies. Hollywood offers entertainment, not art; but that does not mean something inferior, much less something corrupting; it means that the viewer co-operates less submissively, less respecfully, with the performer, the director, the cameraman; he chooses how he will respond, introduces irrelevant and even contrary associations, makes up the total experience according to his own taste. Entertainment, to quote the old tag about romantic art, 'leaves something to the reader's imagination'. This is what Hollywood means to us, quite as much as any doomful writing on the wall.

Now this relaxation and ease of response in the viewer is very similar to what I have called delight and irresponsibility in discussing the writers. Both are characterised by variousness, spontaneity of feeling, and escape from the control of an idea, an imaginative duty, a dominant feeling. Salinger is consciously concerned with this escape.

⸠ "There are nice things in the world – I mean *nice* things. We're all such morons to get side-tracked. Always, always, always referring every goddam thing that happens right back to our lousy little egos." ⸡

Zooey says this, looking at the street in the middle of his discussion with Franny; though all he sees is a girl in a red beret playing with her dog, and the discussion is deadly serious. And Buddy says that a man should be able, if he were lying at the bottom of a hill with his throat cut, bleeding to death, still to raise himself up on one arm if a pretty girl went by, or an old woman with a jar perfectly balanced on her head, and follow her with his eyes over the hill. It is just this, aesthetically, which Salinger and Nabokov achieve; and they do so by accepting, quite profoundly, by feeding on, things like the movies.

The innocent realism of the camera, the extravagance and absurdity of the star system, perhaps above all the humanistic piety of the movies, richly represent those parts of America which these writers have celebrated – have in some sense absorbed. As the thematic climax and solution of 'Zooey' Salinger offers us the idea of the humblest humanity somehow made worthy of our most critical and self-committing love; ordinariness itself made vivid and beautiful. This is a difficult idea to grasp, and a very American one; it is neither British working-class staunchness nor French peasant stoicism; one can think of the grown-up, unglamorous Lolita, with her power of continuing life; but I grasp it best if I think of Sinatra in *Some Came Running*. There (whatever the script may indicate) he played a man bereft of everything that could feed self-esteem, and yet not concerned with his humiliation, not in fact humiliated, merely continuing to want and contrive and get and do without and go away and stay as he is. He is nothing but a human being; but that, he makes us feel, is not primarily a pathetic any more than a proud thing to be; it is what one starts from; and it becomes, to us, a vivid and beautiful thing. Hollywood has always been humanist in this sense. Its treatments of art and religion have not succeeded, but about human relations, especially of the more casual kinds, it has maintained an intelligent piety; just as, about faces, bodies, sexual personalities, it has, in its extravagant and often ridiculous manner, a very sophisticated perception.

Of course Salinger and Nabokov are not the only writers to have made American phenomena ridiculous-and-glamorous; or to have maintained that moviegoer's poise of irreverent-but-filial delight in them. But they are the most talented and serious of those writers; more important, their descriptions of America are thematic; most important, those descriptions make the writers' more private and agonised truths artistically valid. Their new manner introduces into their writing those elements of gaiety and cleverness and energy which save the private agonies from mere claustrophobia and masochism.

Although this picture of the American scene is so irreverent and irresponsible in manner, it includes individuals and whole lives before which the authors are quite naïvely reverent. (In this, as in so much else, American rococo announces its likeness to, perhaps its debt to, Fitzgerald.) What makes the manner so non-participative is just the frustrated exasperation so many people feel at America; the feeling that the good things there have no fixed place, no stable valuation; so that the social picture can be responded to only with indignation (which has grown stale) or with spectator-appreciation, as a great glittering infuriating kaleidoscope, including diamonds among its bottle caps and broken mirrors, but whose only principle of design is the helpless anger and love of the mind on which it impinges.

Richard Chase has pointed out that for important cultural reasons the American novel has not, like the British novel, achieved its best successes when 'moved by an image of' either moral or social harmony, order, coherence. 'The fact is that many of the best American novels achieve their very being, their energy and their form, from the perception and acceptance not of unities but of radical disunities.' Mr Chase offers us American Gothic as the artistic mode of that success; American rococo would have been more to his purpose.

Studies in Classic American Literature

It has always been easy to see, and say, that D. H. Lawrence's studies of American literature are brilliant; and comparatively easy to say that they are true; the difficult thing has been to define their kind of truth – the kind of book he wrote. That difficulty will perhaps always remain, but now that Lawrence's basic method is becoming something of a model for scholarly books on the subject, it is time to declare one's conviction that whatever it is, it is not literary criticism. There is profoundly interesting, potentially helpful, comment on books the student of literature has particular trouble in reading; but it is comment of a kind ultimately tangential to his discipline and always somewhat at odds with it. You cannot take such a model and, by adding scholarship and subtracting eccentricity, make a useful contribution to literary studies. Adding a professional vocabulary, textual analysis, surveys of criticism, comparisons to other literatures; and transforming the manner of the book into something soberer, more impersonal, more imposing; all this will give you something like recent books on American literature, but it will not give you literary criticism. If you look for certain 'American' themes in everything, and interpret their treatment in terms that embody an extra-literary thesis, you are very unlikely to read successfully from a literary point of view.

This is not to say that Lawrence himself was not a fine critic, or was not using his critical gifts in this book. He gives us the great passages, he shows us what the language is doing, he defines his authors' essential quality. His pages have a hundred hints that help us in literary criticism; but his chapters are not literary criticism themselves; because the author is not concerned with a text's total meaning, and value, considered as that kind of text. A literary critical essay may of course discuss only one feature of a poem; but it is bound to take account of the whole thing, bound to read that part in its relation to the totality. Lawrence is not so bound. He ignores the other meanings of, for instance, Poe's 'Ligeia', the other equally relevant ways you can respond to those pages; he defines one meaning so boldly, so independently, that there can be no question of his exaggerating its relative importance; he is not *offering* to consider it in relation to the whole; and therein he is not offering critical comment. Moreover, a critical essayist is bound to read a poem primarily, and ultimately, in order to evaluate it as a poem; bound to judge its problems, and therefore its achievements, in terms that are radically, though not exclusively, formal. This again Lawrence is not bound to do. Having a keen critical sense, his original response to his authors was strongly affected by such considerations; but what he does with that response in these essays, the interpretation he puts on it, is not controlled by them. Indeed, his original response was not so *controlled*. You can see that in the contrast between his comments on Cooper, in earlier and later versions of the studies. In the earlier version he wrote that *The Deerslayer* is 'one of the most beautiful and most perfect books in the world; flawless as a jewel and of gem-like concentration'. In the later: 'It is a gem of a a book. Or a bit of perfect paste. And myself, I like a bit of perfect paste, in a perfect setting, so long as I am not fooled by pretence of reality.' The burden of what he had to say about Cooper remained unchanged; but the evaluation was reversed. This could not happen in literary criticism, because there all response is determined by and towards the evaluation of the individual text. When that changes, everything changes. Lawrence's method was determined by something quite different.

Lawrence was trying to define America as a mode of being; this is what determined his method of discussing novels and poems. He was reading them exclusively for instances of this mode of being. Out of what he found by this examination he constructed a meaning for them. Though he did not, except in rare cases, impose this meaning on them. His essays are *about* the novels and poems they name; only they are not critical accounts of them. But their language does not make this distinction plain. 'Perfect' and 'beautiful' and 'work of art' are used to define non-critical points. Their most famous phrases, 'Never trust the artist. Trust the tale', are widely quoted as the essential licence of all criticism everywhere. But in the meaning their context gives these phrases, that licence is quite unusable by critics. Lawrence is in effect claiming that one can totally discount the author's intention in judging a book; that if a 'symbolic meaning' comes through vividly, the book is a great work of art even if the author's efforts to mean something opposite are quite evident. 'You *must* look through the surface of American art, and see the inner diabolism of the symbolic meaning. Otherwise it is all mere childishness.' This is said in reference to *The Scarlet Letter*; in which Lawrence traces – very convincingly – a symbolic meaning the opposite of that Hawthorne thought he was delivering. Such an allegory may be 'profound and wonderful'; but from a critical point of view such a book cannot be a success. Perhaps theoretically it could be; but this one is not; and I know of no case which is. If an author's mind is so divided in its response to a subject that one part is saying one thing, and another part is secretly and rebelliously saying the opposite, then he is very unlikely to deliver that delicate and difficult structure of meaning we call a work of art. If he delivers the unconscious meaning really vividly, it will be because his conscious mind, his controlling artistry, is not very effective. That is why Hawthorne's treatment of sexual themes is more to Lawrence's purpose than, for instance, Thackeray's. Lawrence's method can make an identification between the artist and the conscious mind, between 'art-speech' and the unconscious, because it is not directed towards critical evaluation but towards prophetic interpretation; hence 'Never trust the artist. Trust the tale'; but literary studies cannot afford that identification. It is perhaps the characteristic twentieth-century literary heresy; formulated in reaction against the opposite nineteenth-century Flaubertian heresy; but no successful literary critic has ever put it into practice. There must be a harmony between the voluntary, conscious, and rational qualities, and their opposites, in any successful work of art.

But if it is not a critical, it is still a literary point of view from which Lawrence's book discusses its authors. In this it resembles Van Wyck Brooks's *America's Coming-of-Age*, and Constance Rourke's *American Humor*, and indeed several of George Orwell's essays on literature. Everything these writers say is interesting to a student of literature perhaps more than to anyone else; much is directly relevant to the act of critical reading; but the form and tendency of their comments is not. This is obvious enough, and therefore not dangerous in any case except Lawrence's; but he was a creative genius; he was also a critical talent of a high order; and he approached the greatest authors with the most penetrating and total of judgements. This is what makes his book such difficult reading.

It is a particularly dangerous inspiration for scholars and critics because its eccentricity, its personalness, which is the first thing they dismiss when they construct their own discussions on this model, has a quite essential function. A subject like 'America as a mode of being' has in our culture no specific, objectively defined, discipline. There is no general agreement about how to treat it, which orders of facts to take into account, how to reconcile one order with another, what to subordinate to what. Everyone's account of it necessarily omits considerations which are basic to other people's. Lawrence, for instance, laid special stress on the rôle of 'idealism' in America; but there could be no general agreement on whether this was a more or less valid ordering principle than another writer's stress on Puritanism or on capitalism. This situation is what Lawrence's manner acknowledges; it completes his statements, and enables him both to mean them absolutely and still admit their partiality; and more 'solid' treatments are both feebler and at the same time more pretentious. It is true that there is some hysteria in the book, some total rage and repudiation of life; and some fairly vulgar irritation with Americans; both of these, obviously, could be removed without damage to the book's basic method. But the impudence of the style, the eccentricity of the manner, could not; they are necessary to the book's serious statements. For instance: 'They revel in subterfuge. They prefer their truth safely swaddled in an ark of bulrushes, and deposited among the reeds until some friendly Egyptian princess comes to rescue the babe.' The invitation to picture Lawrence as a friendly Egyptian princess here really helps shape our response to his later interpretations of Whitman and Melville. To put it crudely, it legitimises the liberties he then takes with the texts. Modern scholars have renounced the liberties he took in his style, but the result is that we are outraged by their partiality with their texts.

It would be both pretentious and crude to offer to say exactly where Lawrence's book becomes misleading from our point of view; but some comments on particular chapters may substantiate the claim that one must not, and need not, swallow it whole as literary comment; that one can discriminate in one's response.

The studies are perhaps easiest to appreciate where they are discussing essayists; where the formal considerations are at a minimum, and where the subject is consciously concerned with ideas of the same general kind as Lawrence's; most of all where, as with Crèvecœur, the subject's experience had the same kind of intensity. When the subject is Dana, on the other hand, some disconcerting metamorphoses occur; Lawrence turns what Dana offers as common sense into 'tragic hopelessness'. This is not a gratuitous metamorphosis. Lawrence's interpretation is a relevant comment on Dana's kind of common sense. Dana's book *is* hopeless from the point of view Lawrence has taught us, and which is always relevant; its narrator has no living centre; he resembles the Skrebensky of *The Rainbow*. But on the other hand, Dana's point of view, grey though it is, has some validity; it gives us some impersonal aspects of that voyage which Lawrence's never would; as serious readers, we cannot jettison that truth in the way Lawrence himself could, because our job *is* to respond to the book as a whole. Lawrence throws a strong and illuminating light on Dana, but one we have to supplement before we begin to sketch the object.

Also, though Dana certainly was an idealist in the sense Lawrence indicts him for, he was so to no very marked or remarkable degree. He merely participated like ten thousand others in that mode of being. Lawrence's account of him, read as literary criticism, would imply something much more strikingly and originally idealistic in him.

Most of Lawrence's essay on Crèvecœur is more centrally relevant to our point of view. But it includes one of those assertions which seem simply mistakes in Lawrence's method. After describing animal consciousness, he says: 'Crèvecœur wanted this kind of knowledge. But comfortably, in his head, along with his other ideas and ideals.' This is the point Lawrence makes often about his 'American-woman' characters, of whom Mrs Witt may stand as an example. But what we find in Crèvecœur is a quite different sentimentality. He wanted to believe nature beautiful and innocent, the Red Indians noble and stoic; the other truths about them, including 'animal consciousness', he sometimes vividly *recorded*, but all his mental excitement, all the interference of his will in his emotions, occurred in the service of orthodox eighteenth-century nature worship. The 'American-woman' character can often be felt not far behind the pages of *Studies in Classic American Literature*, and Lawrence is here tying together two examples of his thesis about America which have no organic connexion.

The essay on Franklin offers us an example of a different weakness. Lawrence paints a picture of Franklin destroying Europe.

‘ Directly, at the Court of France, making a small but very dangerous hole in the side of England, through which hole Europe has by now almost bled to death.   ’

(This picture-book language in Lawrence is usually a sign of inner uncertainty, of reliance on sheer rhetoric.)

‘ And indirectly, in Philadelphia, setting up this unlovely, snuff-coloured little ideal, or automaton, of a pattern American. The pattern American, this dry, moral, utilitarian little democrat, has done more to ruin the old Europe than any Russian nihilist. He has done it by slow attrition, like a son who has stayed at home and obeyed his parents, all the while silently hating their authority, and silently, in his soul, destroying not only their authority but their whole existence.   ’

The implication that Franklin's career was inspired by any such hatred of Europe is either too allegorical, too unsubstantial, too thin to be meaningful, or else too preposterous to be entertained. We cannot believe in such motives, however unconscious, if they do not announce themselves by more effects in the personality. Here Lawrence has over-extended his idea, and trusted to the glamour of his rhetoric to cover the weakness of his thesis.

When we come to the discussion of novelists and poets, we find the same critical traps. Thus the conjuring up of 'Pacific civilisations' in the essay on Melville, though amazingly beautiful, remains as ingenious and rhetorical as the theory of history just mentioned. The idealism diagnosed in Cooper's white novels is no more specially his than it was Dana's; Hawthorne's symbolic betrayal of sentimentality in sex is scarcely more vivid than Cooper's; and the discussion of Poe, like that of Crèvecœur, becomes unconvincing when Lawrence ascribes to him the passion to 'know and understand'. This idea, so vivid and incisive in relation to the Mrs Witt character, becomes quite vague and forceless if attributed also to the narrator of 'Ligeia'. This man's frenzy to 'understand' is something we interpret in part Romantic, part Freudian, not at all Lawrentian terms. Lawrence quotes 'Toutes ses dents étaient des idées' from 'Berenice'; where the hero goes to the tomb of his beloved and pulls out all her thirty-two small white teeth, which he then carries everywhere with him in a box; and Lawrence comments: 'Then they are little fixed ideas of mordant hate, of which he possesses himself.' But our response to that image surely involves more *crudely* sexual feelings than that; Lawrence's imagination worked always in terms of moral ideas, however much unconscious energy it included in them; terms which apply to Mrs Witt much more convincingly than to 'Berenice'.

It is necessary to point all this out only because Lawrence was such a fine critical sensibility; because the essays on Melville and Whitman especially, but indeed all of them, extend and organise one's deepest responses to the texts. *Studies in Classic American Literature* offers us quite invaluable insights into American literature; we are bound to keep re-reading it; and we are likely to get confused by its different kinds of statement. There is only too much evidence in recent scholarship of such confusion. Let us cite only the support critics of Hawthorne have drawn from Lawrence's chapter on *The Scarlet Letter*. The 'duplicity' Lawrence pointed out in the novel is now quite generally and complacently referred to – taken to describe a rich ambiguity, a strong tension between its different meanings. But it in fact describes a weakness of meaning; one part of the book contradicts, makes nonsense of, the other. Lawrence praised *The Scarlet Letter* exclusively as a parable. He made no enthusiastic quotations from Hawthorne's pages like those from Melville's and Dana's. His excitement was aroused by the way *The Scarlet Letter*'s symbolic meaning so completely contradicts the writer's intention, and thus guarantees its own sincerity. This is its 'duplicity'. The more 'wonderful and profound' it is from Lawrence's point of view (as an unconscious parable) the worse it is from ours (as a work of art). This misreading is always being invoked in modern accounts of American literature in general. One analysis of the American novel credits Lawrence with pointing out its 'deep "duplicity" or ironic indirection'; but ironic indirection is almost the last thing Lawrence meant by duplicity; he was talking about literature from a quite different point of view.

Studies in Classic American Literature is a brilliant and successful book, but it has an acute pathos. Lawrence's thesis about America is convincing enough to sustain all the book's demands on our attention and admiration, but as it proceeds, and as we reflect on it, our sense of its partiality deepens into oppression. This oppression is partly intellectual; we feel how much Lawrence has omitted from consideration, how much any coherent and forceful statement must omit; and partly emotional; we feel the strained intensity of belief that can alone sustain a man in such sweeping rejections and re-shapings of reality. In this, as in so many other areas of life, Lawrence strikes us as the victim of his own intensities, his own honesty, his own logic. Because he lived by certain intuitions (the kind men feel mostly in their personal relations), because he trusted his intelligence only when these intuitions inspired or sanctioned it, he followed up their clues all the way, into areas like world history and ontology and politics, where such intuitions are usually considered invalid.

If those clues led him into conflict with the consensus of educated opinion, he contradicted that consensus. His attitude to America in this book is thus as logical, as unwhimsical, as his attitude to the findings of modern science; and even more like, because so costly, his attitude to the 1914–18 war. It was an immense cost to him, to be intellectually, emotionally, and morally in the wrong, at odds with the whole world. But he knew certain truths, and all the opposition that was brought against them was, by every test he could apply, mere inert opinion.

The truths he lived by are available, though in smaller measure, to all men of acute literary sensibility; most of them, if they live with some intensity, feel that order of truth more than the others (the political, for instance, or the scientific, or the prudential) and feel an opposition between that order and the others. However reluctant to acknowledge it, they feel more of ultimate or religious sanction in such truths; for a hundred years now, literature has tentatively aspired to, and retreated from, the status of prophecy; ever since the Transcendentalists literary men have had to decide, each for himself, how much of this power to claim as his own. Lawrence's career and work is something of an emblem to them, therefore, of honesty and courage, however mistaken some of them may judge it. Such men participate, to greater or less degree, in the modern literary mind; and the pathos of *Studies in Classic American Literature* is the spectacle of that mind straining itself to the utmost and in some important sense failing. It fails not because what it says is irrelevant to the subject; and not because what it says is so angry and self-tortured; but because it is so partial in its truth; because we have such a strong sense that quite opposite formulations and interpretations would be equally valid.

Lawrence is the supreme example of the literary mind trusting itself entirely to its own intuitions, and trying to carve out a full-scale intellectual life for itself, finding its way in history, politics, theology, etc., by the use of them alone. But he is far from the only example. That critical school which attempts to pre-scribe for British culture is another; and that which attempts to diagnose the American psyche is another. Literary sensibility, reaching out from books to the whole range of social-cultural phenomena, does give one insights into these problems; but those insights do not make up a total account; they do not even make up a satisfactory skeleton and scaffolding for other kinds of insight to fill in. Social problems have a complexity which no analysis by literary sensibility alone can resolve; though they cannot be resolved *without* the co-operation of that sensibility. But by itself a 'literary' scrutiny of a whole culture reveals only fragments of a pattern; join them together, fill in the intervening spaces according to the pattern, and you falsify.

Lawrence's thesis was that America is a place where the old spirit of Europe is being destroyed; both by an insidious, imitative betrayal, and by the formation of a new spirit, colder, harder, more isolated. The process of betrayal is illustrated in *The Scarlet Letter*; the new spirit in the Chingachgook–Natty Bumppo relation-ship. There is a good deal in American literature and history which this thesis explains. 'The essential American soul is hard, isolate, stoic, and a killer.' This, said of Natty Bumppo, is a remarkable foreshadowing of the heroes of Hemingway and Faulkner. However, it needs no proving that there is a great deal which it does not cover – there are the heroes of Fitzgerald and Salinger. And if, as this book claims, the latter are equally important manifestations of American life, equally the 'essential American soul', then that soul is a free, multiform, varying entity, taking at certain times certain forms to which Lawrence's analysis applies, but taking also quite opposite ones. The American soul, like the British or any other soul, is a potentiality for certain modes of being rather than others; but among these American modes there is great variety and even opposition; idealism, geniality, emotionality, life-giving, these are just as genuinely American as their opposites. To ignore them in one's account of the literature, in effect to reject them in one's reading of it, is to betray the whole spirit of literary studies. This is even more clearly true of the history, the philosophy, the politics. Lawrence's intuition discovered fragments of a pattern in all American culture; he then arbitrarily joined them up; and modern scholars are now following his example. Even the particular patterns they trace follow his. He had intended to call his essays in their first version, 'The Transcendental Element in American Literature'; and the attack on that element is what unites all subsequent criticism. The accusation, and even more the anger, is handed on from critic to critic without real modification. When Allen Tate sketches in nineteenth-century cultural history, *à propos* of Emily Dickinson, he quotes an earlier account: ' "When Emerson had done his work", says Mr Robert Penn Warren, "any tragic possibilities in that culture were dissipated." ' And an arbitrariness, a partiality, we can for many reasons accept in a book like *Studies in Classic American Literature*, becomes a major weakness in an established school of literary studies.

The literary mind's best work on non-literary material, including cultural theory, is always marred by partiality, arbitrariness, and a kind of feebleness. It should never be allowed to dominate, to dictate to, the fuller activity that mind achieves on its native ground, face to face with a book. But that is what this modern literary method in effect permits. Let us take the picturesque example of national types. In *America's Coming-of-Age*, Van Wyck Brooks has a lot to say about the impoverishment of physique in American intellectuals as compared with English. After 'the jocund aspect of young England in flannels' at Oxford, he found some American Rhodes scholars there, 'pallid and wizened, little old men they seemed, rather stale and flat and dry, and I said to myself, it is a barren soil these men have sprung from'. He, and Lawrence too, describes intellectual Americans generally as nerve-worn and pale, sallow and lanky and dry; such impressions are half the evidence (the evidence they *offer*) for their generalisations about American culture. Nowadays both writers would almost certainly draw some quite opposite picture. The lesson of the change is that all such insights, however vivid, are not really valid; and that any *system* of interpretation based on them must fail. Brooks and Lawrence were not systematic; their judgements on both men and books sprang from sharply separate experiences, connected later by the writer's reflection, and hence not dependent one on another; but more academic minds work more logically. The original experiences, in any systematic account, in any work of scholarship, will be partly *controlled* by their logical functions; books will be read *for* their evidence of American 'barrenness'. There are examples enough of this in the critical readings I have disagreed with earlier in this book.

Another similar case is the very general nineteenth-century theory – shared by both English and American writers – that the latter race as a whole was markedly smaller and lighter than the former. Hawthorne, Emerson, Lowell, all repeat this with the excitement of personal conviction; that Americans were less solid, less heavy, less physical, than Englishmen of their own time, and than they themselves used to be – that this was a progressive tendency in Americans. It is clear enough now both that this is not true, and that for all the intelligence and intensity of those observers, their method, their kind of mind, was not adequate to produce a satisfactory total account of such phenomena. And yet just such accounts form the filters through which modern critics see American literature. In everything they read they look for 'America', whichever ideas they include under that heading, and by whatever processes they acquired them. Thanks to a mistaken critical theory, the partiality, arbitrariness, and feebleness of the literary mind at work on foreign material is now allowed to cramp its powers even on home ground.

At another point Brooks deplores the decay of American childhood. Children are now taught that they 'cannot be up and doing too soon'; so that whereas Whitman and Hawthorne were able to mature 'because they had given themselves for so long to life before they began to react upon it', such men will not be seen again. There is no need to argue how unconvincing this is; American childhood can just as well be described as too protected; my point is the easy way the author slips into that apocalyptic view of history which seems to be irresistible to the modern literary mind.

'Once the ordered framework that controlled and directed the political vision of John Adams, Cooper, and even of Jefferson, is rejected, we are confronted by a breed of nineteenth-century Titans whose offspring is ultimately degraded to the "common man" of the twentieth century. '

This example comes from Marius Bewley, who in another place ends an analysis of the decay of taste among the rich with: 'Contemporary men of property have no literary preferences at all. No doubt if they ever read books . . .'

This is one example of that complex of presuppositions about modern culture which make the current theories of American literature plausible. We have heard it from so many distinguished literary men – from all our masters. We ourselves practically never deny it. And yet I would say that no more than half of us effectively believe it. The rest of us live as if there were as much evidence of an equilibrium as a regress, or at least as if the evidence were far too confused to support such a theory. But in the world of ideas we rest under the domination of the old myth – because it seemed so vividly true to our masters. In our discouraged mood we recur to its rich phrasing, and thereby dignify that mood and depreciate its opposite. It distorts our expression and to some extent our experience. In just the same way – and partly in consequence – we accept a theory of American literature which distorts our response to what is there. We accept a habitual antipathy to Emerson, and a habitual sympathy with Hawthorne – habits which are handed on from critic to critic and from reading to reading until they become in effect articles of faith. My case is that those readings no longer really satisfy us, and that it is time to challenge some of the cultural presuppositions of this literary taste.

We are, or claim to be, still reacting against philistine heresies of the inevitability of progress, of the profundity of Transcendentalism, of the innocence of the American temperament. But the books that publish our antitheses to these views are read almost exclusively by ourselves, who need no such antidote. Our bias is quite the other way. And whatever duty we may owe others to contradict their ideas, we owe ourselves a more pressing duty to validate our own – not to surrender our minds to the rigidity of an exaggeration – to derive our ideas always from our experience of the books we are reading. Emerson was a highly intelligent man, even if he was a Transcendentalist; Hawthorne was not, and was a bad writer, even if he did reject nineteenth-century optimism; Faulkner was a minor talent, even if he did deal in violence and myth; Salinger is a brilliant talent, even if he is 'innocent'. We are at the end of a period in literary taste; whether we are at the beginning of a new one depends on whether we can change our categories.

Select Bibliography

Chapter 1

Aldridge, John W. *After the Lost Generation:* a critical study of the writers of two wars. New York 1951

Bewley, Marius *The Complex Fate:* Hawthorne, Henry James, and others, with an introduction and two interpolations by F. R. Leavis. London 1952 *The Eccentric Design:* form in the classic American novel. London 1959

Brooks, Van Wyck *Three Essays on America* New York 1934

Chase, Richard V. *The American Novel and its Tradition* Toronto 1958

Cowley, Malcolm *The Literary Situation* New York 1954

Feidelson, Jr, Charles, and Brodtkorb, Paul, edd. *Interpretations of American Literature* New York 1959

Fiedler, Leslie A. *An End to Innocence:* essays on culture and politics. Boston 1955. *Love and Death in the American Novel* New York 1960

Hoffman, Frederick J. *The Twenties:* American writing in the post-war decade. New York 1955

I'll Take My Stand: the South and the agrarian tradition; by twelve southerners. New York 1930

Kazin, Alfred *On Native Grounds:* an interpretation of modern American prose literature. New York 1942

Lawrence, D. H. *Studies in Classic American Literature* New York 1923

Leavis, F. R. *Pudd'nhead Wilson:* a tale by Mark Twain with an introduction by F. R. Leavis. London 1955

Rourke, Constance *American Humor:* a study of the national character. New York 1931

Styron, William *Set This House on Fire* New York 1960

248

Chapter 2

Emerson, R. W. *The Journals*, 1820-72: ed. E. W. Emerson and W. E. Forbes. Boston 1909-14

Lowell, J. R. *The Biglow Papers* Boston 1859

Matthiessen, F. C. *American Renaissance:* art and expression in the age of Emerson and Whitman. Toronto 1941

Perry, Bliss, ed. *The Heart of Emerson's Journals* New York 1859

Spiller, Robert E., ed. and others *The Literary History of the United States* New York 1948

Woodberry, George *Ralph Waldo Emerson* New York 1907

Chapter 3

Arvin, Newton *The Heart of Hawthorne's Journals* Boston 1929

Hawthorne, Nathaniel *Twice-Told Tales* Boston 1837. *The House of the Seven Gables* Boston 1851. *The Scarlet Letter* Boston 1850. *The Marble Faun* Boston 1860. *The Blithedale Romance* Boston 1852. *Septimius Felton* Boston 1872

Levin, Harry *The Power of Blackness* New York 1958

Stewart, Randall *Nathaniel Hawthorne:* a biography. New Haven 1948

Van Doren, Mark *Nathaniel Hawthorne* New York 1949

Chapter 4

Chase, Richard V. *The American Novel and its Tradition* Toronto 1958

Eliot, George *Middlemarch* Edinburgh 1871-2

James, Henry *The Awkward Age* London 1899

Lawrence, D. H. *Women in Love* New York 1920

Melville, Herman *Moby Dick* New York 1851. *Mardi* New York 1849. *Redburn* New York 1849. *Pierre* New York 1852. *The Piazza Tales* New York 1856

Chapter 5

Chase, R. V. *Walt Whitman Reconsidered* New York 1955

Cooper, James Fenimore *Satanstoe* New York 1845

James, Henry *The Bostonians* London 1886

Lynn, Kenneth *Mark Twain and South-Western Humor* Boston 1960

Thoreau, Henry *Walden* Boston 1854

Twain, Mark *Life on the Mississippi* Boston 1883. *Notebook* New York 1935. *The Adventures of Huckleberry Finn* New York 1885. *The Adven-

tures of Tom Sawyer Hartford 1876. *The Mysterious Stranger* New York
1916. *A Connecticut Yankee at King Arthur's Court* New York 1889

Whitman, Walt *Leaves of Grass* Brooklyn 1855

Chapter 6

James, Henry *The Europeans* London 1878. *Washington Square* New
York 1881. *The Portrait of a Lady* London 1881. *The Bostonians* London
1886. *What Maisie Knew* London 1898. *The Awkward Age* London
1899. *The Complete Tales of Henry James* London 1962

Leavis, F. R. *The Great Tradition:* George Eliot, Henry James, Joseph
Conrad. London 1948

Trilling, Lionel Introduction to *The Bostonians.* Chiltern Library.
London 1952

Chapter 7

Chase, Richard V. *The American Novel and its Tradition* Toronto 1958

Kazin, Alfred *The Stillness of 'Light in August':* Interpretations of American
Literature, ed. Charles Feidelson, Jr, and Paul Brodtkorb. New York 1959

Faulkner, William *As I Lay Dying* New York 1930. *The Sound and the
Fury* New York 1929. *Light in August* New York 1932

Chapter 8

Salinger, J. D. *The Catcher in the Rye* Boston 1951. *Nine Stories* Boston
1953. 'Raise High the Roofbeam, Carpenters'. *The New Yorker*, Vol. 31
(Nov 19, 1955), pp 51 ff. *Franny and Zooey* Boston 1961. 'Introducing
Seymour'. *The New Yorker*, Vol. 35 (June 6, 1959), pp 42 ff

Steiner, George 'The Salinger Industry'. *The Nation* (Nov 14, 1959), p 341

Chapter 9

Eliot, T. S. *Selected Essays* London 1932

Lawrence, D. H. *The Lost Girl* London 1920

Nabokov, Vladimir *Lolita* Paris 1955. *Laughter in the Dark* New York
1938. Rev. ed. New York 1960

Chapter 10

Lawrence, D. H. *The Symbolic Meaning:* the uncollected versions of 'Studies
in Classic American Literature': ed. Armin Arnold. Arundel 1962. *Studies
in Classic American Literature* New York 1923

Kazin, Alfred *The Stillness of 'Light in August':* Interpretations of American
Literature, ed. Charles Feidelson, Jr, and Paul Brodtkorb. New York 1959

Faulkner, William *As I Lay Dying* New York 1930. *The Sound and the
Fury* New York 1929. *Light in August* New York 1932

70
71
72
74
75
76
77
79
80
83
85
89